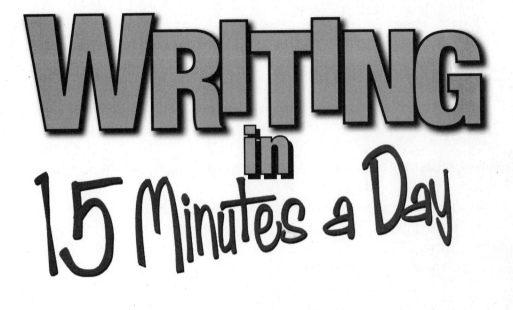

WRITING
in
15 Minutes a Day

LEARNINGEXPRESS®

NEW YORK

Published in the United States by LearningExpress, LLC, New York.

Library of Congress Cataloging-in-Publication Data:
Junior skill builders : writing in 15 minutes a day.
    p. cm.
  Includes bibliographical references.
  ISBN: 978-1-57685-663-5
  1. English language—Composition and exercises—Study and teaching
(Middle school) 2. English language—Composition and exercises—Study
and teaching (Secondary) I. LearningExpress (Organization) II. Title:
Writing in 15 minutes a day.
  LB1631.J87 2008
  808'.0420712—dc22   2008020198

Printed in the United States of America

10 9 8 7 6 5 4 3 2

First Edition

For more information or to place an order, contact LearningExpress at:
  2 Rector Street
  26th Floor
  New York, NY 10006

Or visit us at:
  www.learnatest.com

C O N T E N T S

  - Suggestions for publishing your work—for example, in your
    school newspaper, in a local 'zine, on Internet sites such as your
    school website or online student writing magazine, on Facebook,
    on YouTube, by entering a contest, the possibilities are endless

❶ ❷ ❸ ❹ ❺ ❻ ❼ ❽ ❾ ❿ ⓫

CONGRATULATIONS ON YOUR DECISION to improve your writing skills. By purchasing this book, you have made a very smart move. Being able to write well is probably the single most important skill that you will learn during all your years of school. Writing well is a skill that will last; once you learn how to write, you'll know how forever.

Writing is not only something you need to do for your school work. Writing is a skill that has practically universal uses: It will help you complete all sorts of tasks with greater ease. For example, writing will help you do better on school assignments, send funnier and faster IMs and text messages to your friends, write nicer thank-you notes to your grandparents, and get a better job (and keep it) when you grow up and have to start working.

The importance of writing well may not seem immediately obvious to you, but stop and think about how practically every profession you can think of demands some writing as an everyday part of the job. You may not end up being a newspaper reporter or a famous poet, but in almost any profession you choose, you'll need to know how to write. Imagine how important it is for a pilot to write a clear flight plan. Think about how police officers have to write precise and clear reports about crime scenes. Consider how scientists have to create detailed reports of their experimental findings.

Everyone—and anyone—will find that the ability to write is one of the most important skills to acquire. And the best part is that once you learn how to write, once you've acquired an understanding of the basics of writing, you'll never have to worry about it again. Writing will be like riding a bike—you'll do it naturally, without thinking about it.

"But what about grammar?" you ask. Isn't writing just the same as grammar? If I know grammar, won't I be able to write? And isn't grammar about the most boring subject in the world? Well, the truth is, grammar and writing are indeed closely related. And it's true that you can't do one without the other. If you haven't got a fairly good grasp of grammar, you'll never be at ease as a writer.

But don't get nervous. Grammar is not The Enemy. Instead, grammar is simply the set of rules that enable communication—either spoken or written. And you already know a lot of grammar without even realizing it. When you speak, you automatically construct grammatical sentences. That is, you put together a string of words that convey your meaning. And you do this naturally, usually without stopping to think about it.

Sometimes you haven't spoken clearly, and your friend or your mom or your teacher asks you to clarify. How many times a day does that happen to you? If it happens a lot, you probably just need to slow down. When you write, the same communication (or grammar) rules apply, but because you are writing more slowly, with more care than you apply when you speak, the rules of grammar sometimes poke their heads up and demand consideration.

Writing is generally more formal than speaking, but that doesn't mean writing has to be stuffy and uninteresting. Stop and think about how much of what you do or listen to or watch, is, one way or another, written. What about the songs you listen to? The TV shows and movies you watch? The school books you read? They've all been written. And remember the video games you play. Someone, somewhere, has been writing all that, and you've been receiving this communication one way or the other. So writing is not just something teachers demand; it's a part of everyday life. Being able to write well means being able to communicate effectively, and certainly that's something you already know you want to do. So let's get started.

HOW TO USE THIS BOOK

This book provides a step-by-step guide to improving your writing in just 15 minutes a day. It's that easy! If you devote that very small amount of time each day to reading and absorbing each lesson's material, and completing its short practice exercises, you will definitely become a better writer. Now, doesn't that sound workable? And painless?

The book is divided into 30 lessons, each of which will take you approximately 15 minutes to complete. Each lesson includes short practice exercises that will help you make sure you have understood the lesson. This means that in one month you can become a better writer. Each lesson focuses on a particular skill, or a specific set of concepts that all good writers know and use. The book functions best if you work through it in order, because each lesson builds on the skills developed in earlier lessons. However, once you become a proficient writer, you may find that you follow the steps to good writing in a different order from the one the book suggests. For now, follow the lessons in order, and notice how you begin to feel just a little more confident each day.

You will notice that the book's lessons assume that you are assigned to write an essay, but the process of planning, organizing, and completing a piece of writing are the same if you are writing a song, a poem, a play, or a movie script. Because most readers of this book are students, the book simplifies by giving instructions for essay writing. You can adapt these essay strategies, tricks, and tips to any writing you will do now or in the future. (Ask your parents about what writing they do in their jobs. They may want to use the book's lessons along with you to help in their own writing tasks at work.)

Here are the conditions and supplies you'll need to improve your writing with this book:

- Peace and quiet. No iPod, no TV, no texting or instant messaging. You need to concentrate exclusively on each lesson for 15 minutes if you are really going to improve.
- Pencil and paper. If you want to do the writing exercises on the computer, that's fine. But turn off your browser; no multitasking or web surfing allowed during these 15-minute work sessions.
- A *quiet* kitchen timer. Setting a timer and not interrupting your concentration will ensure that you spend your full 15 minutes on the lesson. And sometimes a lesson will ask you to write without stopping (or thinking) for five minutes, so you may need to time yourself.
- A serious commitment to improving your writing. That's the most important thing you can bring to this effort. Writing well is not magic; it's a skill you can acquire. With this book and only 15 minutes a day of work, you'll soon feel confident and proud of your new skills—you'll really become a good writer!

TIP: Probably the single most effective way to improve your writing doesn't involve writing at all! The secret: READ!

If you read (at least) 15 minutes a day, every day, your writing will (almost magically) improve.

So read—anything. Books. Newspapers. Magazines. Internet sites. Without realizing it, you will absorb new vocabulary words, new sentence structures, new information. All these will enhance your ability to write when you sit down to a writing task.

P R E T E S T

THIS PRETEST CONTAINS 30 questions that will test your knowledge of the topics that will be covered in this book. The test should take about 30 minutes to complete. It will provide you with an accurate sense of your existing knowledge of grammar and writing, and serve as a guide to which areas of these subjects you need to learn better.

The answer key on page 11 provides the lesson number in which each question's topic is discussed.

PRETEST

1. Every sentence you write must include, at the very least, which of the following parts?
   a. subject, predicate, and object
   b. noun as a subject
   c. subject and predicate
   d. noun and pronoun

2. Proper nouns are the parts of speech that
   a. must always be capitalized.
   b. always describe people.
   c. always begin the sentence.
   d. can be mistaken for verbs.

3. The most important function of verbs in most sentences is
   a. to explain who is doing the action.
   b. to describe the action.
   c. to help define the subject.
   d. to complete a sentence.

4. Which word is often used as a helping verb?
   a. be
   b. am
   c. was
   d. has

5. Adverbs are words that modify which parts of speech?
   a. verbs, adjectives, or other adverbs
   b. pronouns and nouns
   c. nouns and verbs
   d. verbs only

6. Which sentence uses the correct predicate?
   a. The dog walk quickly.
   b. The cat purred softly.
   c. The snake done slither.
   d. The kangaroos has jumped.

7. Which of the following word groups is a sentence fragment?
   a. Writing well is often difficult for students.
   b. But learning to write essays and poems.
   c. Driving a car is also difficult to learn.
   d. Running a marathon is perhaps the most difficult of all.

8. Which of the following sentences is a complex sentence?
   a. While tapping her foot, the teacher demanded the students get to work.
   b. The boys ran and the girls hopped.
   c. The rules of English grammar are rarely the favorite topic of most classrooms.
   d. James tried very hard to succeed at completing the test quickly.

9. Which of the following word groups is a dependent clause?
   a. Nancy fell sound asleep.
   b. At seven o'clock in the morning.
   c. The teacher kept talking.
   d. Exercising is exhausting.

10. Which of the following word groups is an independent clause?
   a. Sammy loved pickles more than he loved salami.
   b. When Jeannie made the sandwiches.
   c. If she made them properly.
   d. Eating pickles and ice cream.

11. Which of the following is a correct definition of a compound-complex sentence?
   a. two independent clauses joined by *and*
   b. two independent clauses and one dependent clause
   c. one independent clause and one dependent clause
   d. one independent clause and two dependent clauses

12. Which sentence below is correctly punctuated?
   a. The day after tomorrow, luckily, is the day we will take the test.
   b. The day after tomorrow, luckily; is the day we will take the test.
   c. The day after tomorrow; luckily is the day we will take the test.
   d. The day after tomorrow luckily is the day we will take the test.

13. Which sentence below contains a grammatical error?
- **a.** The boys in the class wanted to eat there lunch at 11:30 A.M.
- **b.** The girls in the class wanted them to sit quietly for another 30 minutes.
- **c.** The teacher told her class to stop fighting over such a silly issue.
- **d.** The lunch hour got to be a very important topic for all of them.

14. Which of these sentences uses pronouns correctly?
- **a.** Who is the best speller in the class?
- **b.** The teacher told me and her to go to the white board.
- **c.** My aunt is whom I like best of all the relatives.
- **d.** My aunt invited him and I to go to the movies.

15. Which of these sentences is correctly punctuated?
- **a.** Smiling sweetly, the teacher explained the assignment, including its due date.
- **b.** Smiling, sweetly the teacher explained the assignment including its due date.
- **c.** Smiling sweetly the teacher explained; the assignment including its due date.
- **d.** Smiling sweetly, the teacher explained, the assignment including its due date.

16. The best place for an essay's thesis statement is
- **a.** in the second or third paragraph.
- **b.** in the first or second paragraph.
- **c.** in the last paragraph.
- **d.** wherever it makes the most sense.

17. Determining the identity of your reader is important because
- **a.** knowing will help you get a better grade.
- **b.** knowing will help you write with more focus.
- **c.** knowing will help you write faster.
- **d.** knowing will help you establish your point of view.

18. All essays should contain
- **a.** at least three paragraphs.
- **b.** five paragraphs.
- **c.** as many as the writer determines is appropriate.
- **d.** as many as the assignment specifies.

19. An introduction should contain
- **a.** background information.
- **b.** a lively anecdote.
- **c.** a thesis statement.
- **d.** a welcoming statement.

20. Which is the correct order of steps in the writing process?
- **a.** brainstorming, drafting, revising
- **b.** planning, revising, editing
- **c.** brainstorming, editing, revising
- **d.** planning, proofreading, editing

21. Which is a correct definition of a thesis?
- **a.** the way a writer introduces an essay
- **b.** an essay that is 350–500 words long
- **c.** the main idea of an essay
- **d.** the prompt for an essay

22. Support for your essay can come from
- **a.** personal experience.
- **b.** interviews.
- **c.** both **a** and **b**
- **d.** none of the above

23. Which of the following is a major benefit of writing an outline?
- **a.** An outline will help you figure out what you think.
- **b.** An outline will tell you how long your essay should be.
- **c.** An outline will help you find grammatical errors.
- **d.** An outline will let you know if your thesis is workable or weak.

24. What is the most common essay organizational pattern?
- **a.** main idea, arguments for and against, conclusion
- **b.** introduction, body, conclusion
- **c.** introduction, comparison and contrast, solution
- **d.** main idea, examples, conclusion

25. Which of these is the correct definition of an expository essay?
- **a.** Expository essays explain the differences between two things.
- **b.** Expository essays are personal essays.
- **c.** Expository essays explain a topic or a process.
- **d.** Expository essays ask questions and then answer them.

26. The conclusion of an essay should
   a. restate the introduction's main idea.
   b. provide a new strong idea.
   c. leave the reader wondering.
   d. suggest a future topic.

27. Writing a first draft should occur when?
   a. before identifying your conclusion
   b. before doing interviews
   c. before settling on a thesis
   d. after writing an outline

28. What is the main problem in the following sentence?
   > The teacher handed out the test papers before she told us what we were supposed to write in the essay it was part of the standardized test that every grade has to take.
   a. It is not punctuated correctly.
   b. It lacks a main idea.
   c. It uses more words than it needs to.
   d. It is a run-on sentence.

29. Which of the answer choices best describes the problem with the following paragraph?
   > Global warming is an important subject. Plants and animals are disappearing or dying. The atmosphere is really polluted, and we need to pay attention.
   a. poor punctuation
   b. lack of sentence structure variety
   c. lack of complex sentences
   d. grammatical errors

30. How would you describe the organizational strategy of the paragraph from question 29?
   a. chronological
   b. exposition of ideas
   c. general to specific
   d. compare and contrast

ANSWERS

1. c (Lesson 1)
2. a (Lesson 1)
3. b (Lesson 1)
4. d (Lesson 1)
5. a (Lesson 1)
6. b (Lesson 1)
7. b (Lesson 2)
8. a (Lesson 2)
9. b (Lesson 2)
10. a (Lesson 2)
11. b (Lesson 2)
12. a (Lesson 4)
13. a (Lesson 3)
14. a (Lesson 3)
15. a (Lesson 4)
16. b (Lesson 7)
17. b (Lesson 7)
18. c (Lessons 13, 21)
19. c (Lesson 13)
20. a (Lesson 8)
21. c (Lesson 12)
22. c (Lesson 20)
23. d (Lesson 14)
24. b (Lesson 13)
25. c (Lesson 16)
26. a (Lesson 21)
27. d (Lesson 19)
28. d (Lesson 2)
29. b (Lesson 2)
30. c (Lesson 14)

S E C T I O N 1

grammar review

EVERYONE—WELL, *ALMOST* everyone—has the same reaction to the word *grammar*. "Ugh!" All those rules to remember. All those exceptions to all those rules. What could be more boring? Well, boring it may be. But nothing, no, nothing, is more important than having good grammar—in both your speech and in your writing. So take a deep breath and pay attention. The first six lessons of this book provide you with a quick and easy review of the most important grammar principles. If you read carefully and complete the practice exercises, you're certain to gain a much improved grasp of how grammar works, and why having good grammar is so important in your life.

the big four parts of speech

Good writing takes more than just time;
it wants your best moments and the best of you.

REAL LIVE PREACHER,
RealLivePreacher.com WEBLOG, 10-09-04

This lesson is the first of six lessons that provide a review of the rules of English grammar. In this lesson, you will review nouns, adjectives, verbs, and adverbs.

THIS BOOK ASSUMES that you have studied grammar already and that you are an efficient communicator orally, but that you just might need reminding about some of the parts of speech and how they work together to form complete and effective sentences.

Remember, you need good grammar if you're going to communicate successfully—both orally and in written form. So now you can begin with this review of the big four parts of speech.

NOUNS

Every sentence must include, at the very least, a noun and a verb; sometimes these are referred to as the subject and the predicate. They're easy to spot. The **noun** is the person, place, or thing doing the action in the sentence. Nouns can be **common nouns**, such as *boy, girl, dog, cat,* or they can be **proper nouns**, which describe a specific person, place, or thing.

Common Nouns	Proper Nouns
school	Harvard University
mouse	Mickey Mouse
gorilla	King Kong
city	New York City
web browser	Google

Be careful to follow the rules of capitalization. Being accurate about these rules can often make the difference between clarity and confusion in a sentence. Note the difference here:

> John visited the White House.
>
> John visited the white house.

The White House, when capitalized, clarifies for the reader that the writer is referring to the home of the president. Without capitalization, the writer can be describing any house that is painted white.

Common nouns are usually not capitalized, except when they are the first word in a sentence. Proper nouns are always capitalized, except when companies (or persons) have made a point of distinguishing themselves by violating the rules. For example, a famous American poet spelled his name e.e. cummings. And eBay and iPod are familiar words in our culture today.

PRACTICE 1: CORRECTING NOUN SPELLINGS

Find and correct the noun spelling errors in the following sentences.

1. King kong was taken from the jungle to New york city where he eventually met a sad end.

2. Probably the most famous duck in the world is named Donald duck.

3. Thousands of nervous High School Students across america compete to become students at a prestigious University named princeton.

4. The small herd of buffalos in San francisco's golden gate park is a popular tourist Attraction.

5. How many minutes (or hours) each day do you spend listening to your new ipod?

ADJECTIVES

Adjectives are words that describe, modify, specify, or qualify a noun. For example, identify the adjectives in these phrases:

> cool group
>
> boring lesson
>
> nice teacher
>
> interesting book

PRACTICE 2: IDENTIFYING ADJECTIVES

Return to the five sentences from Practice 1 that you corrected for noun spelling and underline the adjectives in each sentence.

VERBS

Verbs are the words that describe the action in a sentence, or that define the relationship between two things. When a verb is doing the action in a sentence, it is called the **predicate**. Verbs also define the time of the action: the present, the past, or the future.

Often verbs are accompanied by helping verbs that serve to define further the time or nature of the action. Here are some common helping verbs:

has	have	had
should	would	could

Can you think of others? Or find others in Practice 3?

PRACTICE 3: IDENTIFYING VERBS AND THEIR TENSES

In the following sentences, identify present and future tense verbs (and their helpers) by circling them and identify past tense verbs (and their helpers) by underlining them. (Be careful: Sometimes verbs can act like nouns.)

1. The dogs barked furiously as the cars frantically whizzed past on their way to the rock concert that will begin at midnight.

2. I laughed uproariously when I realized how nervous I had been about doing well on the geography test.

3. More than two dozen species of animals peacefully inhabit the wildlife preserve.

4. Trudging wearily through a driving snow to school every day used to be a common event in some parts of the Midwest.

5. Prince, whose original name was Prince Rogers Nelson, famously began his musical career during junior high school with a small band called Grand Central.

ADVERBS

Adverbs are words that modify a verb, an adjective, or another adverb. For example, identify the adverbs in these phrases:

singing badly
carefully picking blackberries
sleeping soundly
write easily
vigorously competing to win
gratefully counting blessings

PRACTICE 4: IDENTIFYING ADVERBS

Reread the five sentences from Practice 3 in which you identified verb forms. Look at these sentences again and circle the adverbs in each sentence.

1. The dogs barked furiously as the cars frantically whizzed past on their way to the rock concert that will begin at midnight.

2. I laughed uproariously when I realized how nervous I had been about doing well on the geography test.

3. More than two dozen species of animals peacefully inhabit the wildlife preserve.

4. Trudging wearily through a driving snow to school every day used to be a common event in some parts of the Midwest.

5. Prince, whose original name was Prince Rogers Nelson, famously began his musical career during junior high school with a small band called Grand Central.

VERB-NOUN AGREEMENT

One of the most common writing errors is the failure to make the subject and the predicate (the noun and the verb) in a sentence agree in number. If the subject of the sentence is singular (*a boy*), then the verb must be a singular verb. (The boy walks around the block. The girls walk around the block.) Most often, the error of not matching the subject and predicate correctly is made in haste. There is really no excuse for making this error, especially since it is so easy to correct.

PRACTICE 5: IDENTIFYING CORRECT VERB-NOUN AGREEMENT IN SENTENCES

Fill in the blank with the correct verb form in the following sentences.

1. The mother cat _____ a litter of four striped and two ginger kittens.
   a. had
   b. have

2. While trying to _____ his favorite kitten from the rooftop, Jeremy fell and knocked himself out.

    a. have rescued

    b. rescue

3. We _____ Jeremy fall, and heard a loud thud.

    a. seen

    b. saw

4. The lesson we _____ was a sad one, but also funny.

    a. had learned

    b. learned

5. Cats _____ sometimes a lot smarter than boys about judging distances.

    a. is

    b. are

....

TIP: Before you finalize any piece of writing, go through it one last time to make sure that each verb matches its subject in number, and matches the meaning of the sentence in tense.

....

ANSWERS

Practice 1: Correcting Noun Spellings

1. King Kong was taken from the jungle to New York City where he eventually met a sad end.
2. Probably the most famous duck in the world is named Donald Duck.
3. Thousands of nervous high school students across America compete to become students at a prestigious university named Princeton.
4. The small herd of buffalos in San Francisco's Golden Gate Park is a popular tourist attraction.
5. How many minutes (or hours) each day do you spend listening to your new iPod?

Practice 2: Identifying Adjectives

1. King Kong was taken from the jungle to New York City where he eventually met a <u>sad</u> end.
2. Probably the most <u>famous</u> duck in the world is named Donald Duck.
3. Thousands of <u>nervous</u> high school students across America compete to become students at a <u>prestigious</u> university named Princeton.
4. The <u>small</u> herd of buffalo in San Francisco's Golden Gate Park is a <u>popular</u> <u>tourist</u> attraction.
5. How <u>many</u> minutes (or hours) <u>each</u> day do you spend listening to your <u>new</u> iPod?

Practice 3: Identifying Verbs and Their Tenses

Present and future tenses are circled; past tenses are underlined.

1. The dogs <u>barked</u> furiously as the cars frantically <u>whizzed</u> past on their way to the rock concert that (will begin) at midnight.
2. I <u>laughed</u> uproariously when I <u>realized</u> how nervous I <u>had been</u> about doing well on the geography test.
3. More than two dozen species of animals peacefully (inhabit) the wildlife preserve.
4. Trudging wearily through a driving snow to school every day <u>used to be</u> a common event in some parts of the Midwest.

5. Prince, whose original name <u>was</u> Prince Rogers Nelson, famously <u>began</u> his musical career during junior high school with a small band called Grand Central.

Practice 4: Identifying Adverbs

Adverbs are circled.

1. The dogs barked (furiously) as the cars (frantically) whizzed past on their way to the rock concert that will begin at midnight.
2. I laughed (uproariously) when I realized how nervous I had been about doing well on the geography test.
3. More than two dozen species of animals (peacefully) inhabit the wildlife preserve.
4. Trudging (wearily) through a driving snow to school (every day) used to be a common event in some parts of the Midwest.
5. Prince, whose original name was Prince Rogers Nelson, (famously) began his musical career during junior high school with a small band called Grand Central.

Practice 5: Identifying Correct Verb-Noun Agreement in Sentences

1. **a.** had
2. **b.** rescue
3. **b.** saw
4. **b.** learned
5. **b.** are

sentence structure

Writing is an exploration. You start from nothing and learn as you go.
E. L. DOCTOROW (1931–   )
AMERICAN NOVELIST

This lesson focuses on the various types of sentences and pays particular attention to common sentence errors such as sentence fragments and comma splices.

NOW THAT YOU'VE completed a review of the big four (and most important) parts of speech, this lesson provides a quick review of how those parts of speech function in correct sentence structures.

Don't be put off by technical grammatical terms. Correct sentence structure is simply the term for the ways in which sentences are constructed in proper English. However, you need to remember that spoken English is often more informal than written English. Think of how many times you answer a question by saying, "Yeah, okay." Or you answer with an incomplete phrase like "Not me." Those are incomplete sentences that are acceptable in conversation, but that may not qualify as correct sentences in formal writing. So be aware that when you are writing, 99% of the time you must obey the formal rules of sentence structure.

Basically, sentences are made up of words put together to communicate ideas. Every grammatically correct sentence must have a **subject** (the noun doing the action) and a **predicate** (the verb describing the action). Once words are combined to communicate ideas, they are called **clauses**. And clauses can be either **independent clauses**, which are clauses that express a complete idea, or they can be **dependent** (or subordinate) **clauses**, which are clauses that do not express a complete idea but that contribute to (or modify) the independent clause in a sentence. Once you understand these basic definitions, you should have no problem constructing sentences that convey your ideas grammatically.

THREE KINDS OF SENTENCES

There are three kinds of sentences: simple, compound, and complex. Look at the following samples to see how the three types of sentences differ from each other.

1. **Simple sentence:** Fido loves to greet visitors.
    Simple sentences contain one independent clause that expresses a complete thought.
2. **Compound sentence:** Fido loves to greet visitors, and he often slobbers all over them.
    Compound sentences contain two (or more) independent clauses and no dependent clauses.
3. **Complex sentence:** Because Fido is such a happy dog, many neighbors don't mind his slobbering.
    Complex sentences contain one independent clause and one or more dependent clauses.

Compound-complex sentences are also possible. They combine the two categories, and can contain two or more independent clauses as well as one or more dependent clause. Here is an example of a compound-complex sentence:

Because Fido is such a happy dog, he often slobbers on visitors, and he frequently jumps up frantically to kiss them as well.

TIP: Here are a few simple sentence structure rules:

- Simple sentences are not necessarily short, but they must contain only one independent clause.
- In compound sentences, the two (or more) independent clauses must be related in thought.
- In complex sentences, the dependent clause clarifies the relationship between ideas. Often, these dependent clauses start with words like *because, when, who,* or *where.*

PRACTICE 1: IDENTIFYING SENTENCE STRUCTURE

For each sentence, identify its structure type. Underline independent clauses once. If there are dependent clauses in the sentences, underline them twice.

1. Friendly dogs usually prance around in an attempt to express their glee, and they also often bark a lot.

2. My dog, who is shy and easily frightened, barks most often when she meets strangers.

3. Scaredy-cat dogs are often the loudest barkers.

4. Because scaredy-cat dogs are sometimes fearful, they can be difficult to train.

5. Having a happy, well-behaved dog is one of life's great pleasures.

SENTENCE FRAGMENTS

One of the most common errors that writers make is to write sentence fragments. You absolutely must learn never to make this error. (Other common errors will be discussed later in this lesson.)

Sentence fragments are sentences that lack one or more of their essential elements; they lack either a subject or, more commonly, a predicate (the verb).

How to Avoid Writing Sentence Fragments

Read every sentence you've written aloud, very slowly. If you've written a fragment, you'll hear your voice stop in midair at the end of the sentence. This is because in our natural rhythm of speech, we drop our voices at the end of a sentence, which is usually when the idea of the sentence is complete. Usually when you read a fragment aloud, your voice at the end will sound as if it is dangling off the edge of a cliff.

After reading every sentence aloud, go back through your writing and check each and every sentence to make sure that it falls into one of the three sentence structure categories. Remember, every sentence must have at least one subject and one predicate, and compound sentences can contain two subjects and two predicates.

PRACTICE 2: IDENTIFYING SENTENCE FRAGMENTS

Read the following sentences aloud and see how they sound. Which ones are complete sentences and which ones are sentence fragments?

> Because I am trying to improve.
> Using big words to impress the reader.
> Talking is not so different from writing.
> Writing can be difficult.

Could you tell the difference? The first two are sentence fragments. While both of these fragments contain nouns and verbs, neither of them contains a completed idea or action. If you are still confused, try reading them aloud again. Listen for how your voice dangles; that's the tip-off that these clauses have not completed an idea, and therefore, they do not constitute a complete grammatical sentence.

....

TIP: When are fragments allowed? You will sometimes notice that writers use fragments for effect. (This book sometimes uses fragments, for example.) Fragments are allowed only when they are used carefully, and for dramatic effect or to emphasize a point. As you read, note carefully the use of fragments; analyze why the writer has chosen to ignore the strict rules of grammatical sentence structures. In your own writing, you'll be much safer if you obey the rules.

....

RUN-ON SENTENCES

Another very common error that writers make is to write run-on sentences. These are exactly what they sound like: two or more sentences (or thoughts) that have been jammed together and written as if they were one. You can check your writing for run-ons in the same way you check for sentence fragments: by reading aloud and by making sure that the sentence doesn't attempt to say too much, all in one breath. Complex sentences, as you know, may contain more than one dependent clause, but sentences that contain more than one independent clause must include a connecting word (such as *and* or *because*) in order to be grammatically correct compound sentences. Careless writers include too many separate ideas, strung together with or without connecting words, in a single sentence.

PRACTICE 3: IDENTIFYING RUN-ON SENTENCES

Read the following sentences aloud and see how they sound. Which ones are correct sentences and which ones are run-ons?

1. Computers are very popular gifts for birthdays and holidays most kids love getting them.

2. It would be difficult to find a boy or a girl who wouldn't love to get a computer as a gift.

3. Janey wanted to find a bargain she finally found one on the sale rack.

4. If you do a lot of careful shopping, both in local stores and on the Internet, you can usually find a bargain.

5. Holiday shopping is the time when bargains are easy to find Janey found this to be true.

Were you able to find the run-ons? They are sentences 1, 3, and 5. Sentences 2 and 4 are correct grammatical sentences. Can you now fix the three run-ons and make them into correct sentences? (The answer key at the end of the lesson offers suggestions on how to correct these sentences.)

....

TIP: Here are a few hints on how to avoid common sentence structure errors:

1. Check each sentence you write, carefully, for complete thoughts, and for the appropriate subject-predicate pairs.
2. Read each of your sentences aloud to see if your voice drops naturally at the end of the sentence. If it doesn't, you've probably written a fragment.
3. Slow down. Rushing to get your work finished is a common trap, and very often the rush will produce sentence fragments and/or run-ons.

....

ANSWERS

Practice 1: Identifying Sentence Structure

1. Friendly <u>dogs usually prance</u> around in an attempt to express their glee, and <u>they also often bark</u> a lot.
2. <u>My dog, who is shy and easily frightened, barks</u> most often when she meets strangers.
3. Scaredy-cat <u>dogs are</u> often the loudest barkers.
4. <u>Because scaredy-cat dogs are sometimes fearful,</u> <u>they can be</u> difficult to train.
5. <u>Having a happy, well-behaved dog is</u> one of life's great pleasures.

Practice 3: Identifying Run-On Sentences

1. Computers are very popular gifts for birthdays and holidays. Most kids love getting them.
3. Janey wanted to find a bargain, and she finally found one on the sale rack.
5. Holiday shopping is the time when bargains are easy to find, and Janey found this to be true.

the all-important pronouns

I love being a writer. What I can't stand is the paperwork.
PETER DE VRIES (1910–1993)
AMERICAN NOVELIST

In this lesson, you'll learn about the proper use of pronouns. Pay particular attention to common pronoun errors that too many writers make.

YOU ARE NO doubt aware that there are parts of speech, in addition to the big four, that you need to be especially careful about using. This lesson reviews pronouns, some of the most useful and troublesome little parts of speech. If you want your writing to improve, you must pay close attention to the material in this lesson. Using pronouns correctly is one of the sure signs of an accomplished writer. And using pronouns incorrectly immediately signals that you are not a careful or skillful writer. So pay attention!

PRONOUNS

The proper use of pronouns is a bit complicated, but once you think about them, you'll realize that you use them every day, all the time, without hesitation. The trick is knowing when to use which one of the many pronouns available in our language. A **pronoun** is a word used in place of a noun or of another pronoun. And the word that the pronoun refers to is called its **antecedent**.

There are several categories of pronouns. The ones we use most often, and that you need to pay special attention to, are personal pronouns, possessive pronouns, reflexive and intensive pronouns, and interrogative pronouns. Even given all these different types, the function of the pronoun is always about the same: It replaces another word or group of words.

The grammatical function the pronoun serves in a sentence is called its **case**, which defines whether the pronoun is being used as the subject of the sentence, as the object of another word, or in a possessive or reflexive form.

PERSONAL AND POSSESSIVE PRONOUNS

Personal pronouns are the pronouns that you probably use most often. Here's a chart that categorizes their correct forms:

SINGULAR PERSONAL PRONOUNS

	Subjective	Objective	Possessive
first person	I	me	my, mine
second person	you	you	your, yours
third person	he, she, it	him, her, it	his, her, hers, its

PLURAL PERSONAL PRONOUNS

	Subjective	Objective	Possessive
first person	we	us	our, ours
second person	you	you	your, yours
third person	they	them	their, theirs

The Correct Use of Personal Pronouns

Here are some sample sentences using pronouns, along with explanations of the grammatical function, or case, in which each pronoun is being used.

<u>We</u> ate our pizza faster than the kids at the next table ate <u>theirs</u>.

The plural pronoun *we* is used here as the subject of the sentence; the plural possessive pronoun *theirs* is used to substitute for the implied words *the students' pizza*, and is the object of the verb *ate*.

Ms. Johnson asked all of <u>them</u> to please sit down and be quiet.

The plural pronoun *them* is the object of the preposition *of* and is used to substitute for the implied word *students*.

<u>You</u> told <u>me</u> that <u>your</u> bicycle was faster than <u>mine</u>.

You is a singular pronoun used as the subject of the sentence; *me* is a singular pronoun used as the object of the verb *told*; *your* is a possessive pronoun describing who owns the bicycle; and *mine* is the singular possessive used to explain who owns the bike.

As you can see in these examples, pronouns are extremely useful words. They enable us to communicate quickly, use fewer words, and therefore create less clutter and repetition on the page.

However, personal pronouns are among the most frequently misused words. Why? Probably because speakers (and writers) are being sloppy and not paying attention to the rules they learned in school.

The Proper Use of Emoticons

Emoticons are representations of facial expressions of emotion created by typing a sequence of characters to suggest an expression such as a smile or a frown. If you think about it, emoticons are a kind of pronoun, because they stand for something else. Emoticons were first used as a typing shortcut in the sending of informal e-mails and instant messages, and are perfectly acceptable to use in personal communications. However, they do not belong in formal writing. If used there, they suggest immaturity and lack of seriousness on the part of the writer. It is best not to use emoticons in your published essays, stories, or school papers; instead, save them for more informal conversations with friends.

PRACTICE 1: CHOOSING THE CORRECT PERSONAL PRONOUN

In the following sentences, choose the correct personal pronouns and identify them as subjective or objective pronouns.

1. Our teacher Ms. Prim glared at Tom and (*me, I*).

2. The other kids in the class laughed when (*him and me; he and I*) were sent out of the room.

3. My classmates and I told our parents that (*she, her*) was a terrible teacher and that's why (*we, us*) were getting bad grades.

4. Tom and (*me, I*) got to school late one day, and Ms. Prim made an example of (*we, us*) to the other kids by sending us to Study Hall.

5. My parents and Tom's talked to Ms. Prim and promised that (*he and I; him and me*) would straighten up in the future.

. . . .

TIP: Using the right personal pronoun is one of the hardest lessons for students and adults alike. Study the chart on page 30 carefully until you are sure you know the difference between subjective and objective pronouns. Then, whether you are speaking or writing, try always to consider whether you are using a pronoun as the main subject of the sentence or clause (the person or thing doing the action) or if you are using the pronoun to describe the person or thing having something done or said to them.

. . . .

Special Reminder: The Linking Verb Rule

When a pronoun functions as the object of a linking verb (any form of the verb *to be*, for example, *is, am, are, was, were, been, can be, will be, should be*), you must use the subjective form of the pronoun. This may sound formal and awkward to you, but it is a strict rule, and if you remember to observe this rule, your readers (and listeners) will immediately recognize you as a skilled and educated writer. And that's what you want, right? Here are some correct samples of this usage:

The best player in the band is he.

The fans who adore him are you and I.

The happy manager of the band was she.

....

TIP: A good way to check for accuracy with linking verb sentences is to turn the sentence upside down and see if it sounds right. For example, *He is the best player in the band* sounds right; and *Him is the best player in the band* does not sound right.

....

REFLEXIVE AND INTENSIVE PRONOUNS

You use reflexive and intensive pronouns all the time, even if you don't remember their category names. Here are clear definitions to remind you about them, and to make it easier for you to use these pronouns correctly in the future. Note that they all end in *self* or *selves*.

Reflexive pronouns refer to the subject of the sentence and direct the action of the sentence back to the subject. Reflexive pronouns are always essential to the sentence's meaning.

John Lennon dedicated himself to promoting world peace.

Yoko Ono joined John and called herself a peace advocate.

Intensive pronouns emphasize another pronoun or noun in the sentence.

The Beatles themselves wrote all of their own music.

I myself have always been a devoted fan of Ringo.

....

TIP: If you delete the reflexive pronoun from the sentence, it doesn't make grammatical sense. Intensive pronouns, on the other hand, are not essential to the sentence's meaning.

....

DEMONSTRATIVE PRONOUNS

Demonstrative pronouns (*this, that, these, those*) are fairly easy to use. They demonstrate what you are talking about; they point out a noun. Here are some correct samples:

> This is an easy lesson to learn.
>
> Those other pronouns are much more difficult to get right.

TIP: A common mistake that many writers and speakers make is to double up and add the words *here* or *there*. For example, an inexpert writer might make mistakes like these:

> This here lesson is driving me crazy.
>
> That there assignment is the worst we've ever had.

Be careful not to insert extra words.

THE *THAT–WHICH* CONFUSION

Use the pronoun *that* when what follows it is essential to your sentence. Use the pronoun *which* (with a comma in front of it) when the clause it introduces can be deleted from the sentence without destroying its meaning. For example:

> Careful writing that includes correct pronouns is a sign of good education.
>
> Writing, which is a difficult task, can often be rewarding.

INTERROGATIVE PRONOUNS: IS IT *WHO* OR *WHOM*?

There are several interrogative pronouns, and they're easy to spot. (Remember that the word *interrogative* is related to *interrogation*, a word you probably know from watching too many detective shows on TV.) **Interrogative pronouns** ask *who* and *whom*. Here are examples of the correct usage of *who* and *whom*:

> *Who* is always used as a subject (*who* replaces *he* or *she*).

> Who writes better than I do?
>
> Your favorite Beatle is who? (Linking verb takes a subject.)

Whom is always used as an object (*whom* replaces *him, her,* or *them*).

> With whom are you going to the concert?
>
> You gave whom the answers to this week's math homework?

PRACTICE 2: USING CORRECT PRONOUNS

Choose the correct pronouns in the following sentences.

1. To become a good writer, you need to determine (*what, which*) is your ultimate goal.

2. If you share your homework, to (*whom, whose*) should the teacher award the grade?

3. To (*who, whom*) should you direct your questions about writing?

4. Imagine that (*your, you're*) a famous poet; (*who, whom*) will you thank when you are accepting the Nobel Prize?

5. Surely you will want to thank (*your, you're*) parents for all the support they gave you.

6. My first attempts at poetry made (*their, they're*) way into the trash bin.

7. When writing is going well, (*it's, its*) a true pleasure.

8. Just between you and (*I, me*), I have always hated writing, but I'm beginning to change my mind.

9. Writing students often find (*their selves, themselves*) scratching their heads.

10. My Facebook friend sent an IM to my cousin and (*I, me*).

TIP: Believe it or not, what you should do right now is go back to the beginning of this lesson and read through it carefully one more time. Pronouns are easily confused, and you will benefit in the long run if you spend an extra few minutes reviewing the pronoun rules. And remember to look back at this lesson whenever you find yourself hesitating about which pronoun to use. Good luck!

ANSWERS

Practice 1: Choosing the Correct Personal Pronoun

1. me (objective pronoun)
2. he and I (subjective pronouns)
3. she, we (subjective pronouns)
4. I (subjective pronoun)
5. he and I (subjective pronouns)

Practice 2: Using Correct Pronouns

1. what
2. whom
3. whom
4. you're, whom
5. your
6. their
7. it's
8. me
9. themselves
10. me

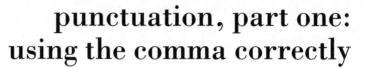

LESSON 4

punctuation, part one: using the comma correctly

I was working on the proof of one of my poems all the morning, and took out a comma. In the afternoon I put it back again.

OSCAR WILDE (1854–1900)
IRISH NOVELIST AND POET

In this lesson, you'll learn how to use the comma, the grammatical device that causes writers more trouble than any other.

HOW DIFFICULT CAN punctuation be? Don't all sentences end in a period? Don't you put a question mark at the end of a sentence that asks a question? And don't you use an exclamation point when you want to convey drama or make a very strong point? What else is there?

Well, there's the comma: the dreaded, evil, nasty comma. The comma is basically the single detail in writing that causes more difficulties and gets writers into more trouble than any other element in the writing process. Commas cause lots more trouble than verbs and pronouns, and they usually beat out the competition from sentence fragments and run-ons for First Prize in Trouble-making. So pay attention here; you can learn to use commas correctly with a lot of thought and a little practice. (We'll review other punctuation marks in the next lesson.)

COMMAS

What are commas for, anyway? Why do we need them? **Commas** are actually very useful grammatical tools: They separate parts of a sentence in order to make meanings clear. It's that simple.

BEWARE THE COMMA SPLICE

You may have seen the term *comma splice* written by your teacher in the margins of your papers. *Comma splice* is the term used to describe the incorrect use of a comma; it is called a splice because the most common error is to splice (or slice) a sentence, dividing two independent clauses with only a comma. Beware the comma splice. It is the most common comma error, and it results from a writer's uncertainty, ignorance about comma rules, or just plain negligence.

....

TIP: When in doubt about a comma, leave it out. You have a better chance of conveying meaning without a comma than you do with sticking one in arbitrarily and thereby splicing the sentence unnecessarily.

....

The Proper Use of Commas

1. Use a comma to join independent clauses in a compound sentence.

    The students got tired of working, but the assignment demanded more time.

    The lessons require some effort, or the students won't learn the right way to write.

2. Use a comma after an introductory phrase or word.

    Finally, the students understood the concept.

    After much complaining, the students liked knowing how to use commas.

3. Use a comma to insert an interrupting element in a sentence, or when the sentence is addressed directly to a person or persons.

> The lesson provided, at long last, a clear way to understand comma rules.
>
> All students, especially you, Andrea, really need to pay attention to your comma usage.
>
> The teacher, Ms. Prim, frequently grows impatient when her students misbehave.

4. Use commas to separate items in a series.

> My favorite fruits are apples, oranges, tangerines, and kiwis.

5. Use commas between adjectives when the adjectives are equal and modify the same noun.

> Our delicious, colorful meals are also nutritious.
>
> (*Our delicious and colorful meals are also nutritious* would also be correct, but why include that extra word?)

Do not use a comma when the adjectives together create a single idea:

> The intense green kiwi is a beautiful—and tasty—fruit.
>
> (The first adjective, *intense*, modifies the second adjective, *green*, rather than the noun *kiwi*. To test whether or not a comma is wanted between two adjectives, insert the word *and* where the comma would be. *The intense and green kiwi* doesn't make sense, so you omit the comma.)

6. Use commas in dates, addresses, and letters.

> September 11, 2001
> New York, New York
> Washington, D.C.
>
> Dear John,
> Sincerely yours,
> Hugs and kisses,

7. Use a comma to avoid confusion.

> **Unclear:** After you study the use of commas will become much clearer.

> **Clear:** After you study, the use of commas will become much clearer.

PRACTICE 1: USING CORRECT PUNCTUATION IN A LETTER

Correct the comma usage in the following letter. If you have questions, refer to the comma usage rules you have just reviewed to help you insert (or delete) commas and other punctuation marks in the appropriate places.

111 W 1111th Street
New York New York 11111
January 1 2008

Dear Lynne

Can you remember what it was like trying to teach students, how to use the comma. I am having a very funny and somewhat frustrating, experience teaching commas to my students because they find the subject incredibly boring. Do you blame them.

Their solution alas to the problem of when to insert a comma is to sprinkle commas throughout their essays as if they were chocolate sprinkles on an ice cream cone. While I like the idea of ice cream I have to point out to them that there are rules that must be followed or the reader will end up very confused. One of my students actually told me that she decided to put them in at a rate of two commas for every other sentence she figured this would make her writing look more "professional."

Do you have any suggestions for how I can make commas more fun. Any advice you can offer will be much appreciated.

Sincerely
Joy

PRACTICE 2: USING COMMAS CORRECTLY

Insert commas in the appropriate places in the following sentences.

1. A long river the Mississippi can be said to divide the United States into two parts west and east.

2. When you are traveling west from Philadelphia you arrive in Chicago long before you arrive in Salt Lake City.

3. "Seeing the country by car" said my tour guide "is really the best way to learn what being an American is all about."

4. Getting to a scheduled airline flight these days can be very difficult due to the requirement that you take off your shoes and jacket throw away your water bottle and show your ticket before you enter the gate area.

5. On the other hand there is no mode of travel that is faster easier simpler and more modern than air flight.

6. Trekking however is actually my favorite way to see the countryside.

7. My family favors camping vacations which include sleeping eating and even showering out in nature.

8. The hazards of camping can include mosquitoes ants and sometimes bears.

9. After being awakened by our first bear we drove to town the very next day and bought a big tent.

10. My mother has always told me that the best education is earned in the following ways: traveling to new places reading good books and conscientiously practicing all the hard grammar rules.

ANSWERS

Practice 1: Using Correct Punctuation in a Letter

111 W. 1111th Street
New York, New York 11111
January 1, 2008

Dear Lynne,

Can you remember what it was like trying to teach students how to use the comma? I am having a very funny and somewhat frustrating experience teaching commas to my students, because they find the subject incredibly boring. Do you blame them?

Their solution, alas, to the problem of when to insert a comma is to sprinkle commas throughout their essays as if they were chocolate sprinkles on an ice cream cone. While I like the idea of ice cream, I have to point out to them that there are rules that must be followed or the reader will end up very confused. One of my students actually told me that she decided to put them in at a rate of two commas for every other sentence. She figured this would make her writing look more "professional."

Do you have any suggestions for how I can make commas more fun? Any advice you can offer will be much appreciated.

Sincerely,
Joy

Practice 2: Using Commas Correctly

1. A long river, the Mississippi can be said to divide the United States into two parts, west and east.

2. When you are traveling west from Philadelphia, you arrive in Chicago long before you arrive in Salt Lake City.

3. "Seeing the country by car," said my tour guide, "is really the best way to learn what being an American is all about."

4. Getting to a scheduled airline flight these days can be very difficult due to the requirement that you take off your shoes and jacket, throw away your water bottle, and show your ticket before you enter the gate area.

5. On the other hand, there is no mode of travel that is faster, easier, simpler, and more modern than air flight.

6. Trekking, however, is actually my favorite way to see the countryside.

7. My family favors camping vacations, which include sleeping, eating, and even showering out in nature.

8. The hazards of camping can include mosquitoes, ants, and sometimes bears.

9. After being awakened by our first bear, we drove to town the very next day and bought a big tent.

10. My mother has always told me that the best education is earned in the following ways: traveling to new places, reading good books, and conscientiously practicing all the hard grammar rules.

punctuation, part two: the other punctuation marks

*The writer who neglects punctuation,
or mispunctuates, is liable to be misunderstood.*
EDGAR ALLAN POE (1809–1849)
AMERICAN POET, CRITIC, SHORT-STORY WRITER

This lesson provides a review of the basic punctuation marks that you must master if you are to become a better writer. Learning to use punctuation marks correctly is probably the simplest part of learning to write well, but that doesn't mean you should skimp on the review or take punctuation lightly.

THIS LESSON FOCUSES on the tiny little punctuation marks that can make all the difference between good writing and sloppy work. Remember, details are always important. As we've seen in the preceding grammar review lessons, the creation of sentences is a process of combining words into sentences that obey certain rules of construction. Those sentence structures are built using a variety of punctuation marks that are more than just an arbitrary set of dots and dashes. Try thinking of each and every sentence you write as a building you are constructing; its punctuation marks create the outer walls and inner hallways that determine the shape and size of the building. Indeed, punctuation marks are as essential to writing well as are correct verbs and coherent thoughts. Your building can easily crumble if its walls are not supported properly.

THE PROPER USE OF THE PERIOD AND OTHER END MARKS

Everyone knows what a period is, but did you know that technically the period is called an *end mark*? Other end marks you must use very carefully are exclamation points and question marks.

Periods, Exclamation Points, and Question Marks

Use a period at the end of **declarative sentences**, those that simply make a statement, unless another punctuation mark is called for.

> It is cloudy today.

Imperative sentences (those that give a command) or **exclamatory sentences** or **phrases** (those that express a strong idea) often end with an exclamation mark.

> Be careful! That floor is very slippery!
> Yikes! I had forgotten to tell my mother what time I'll be home.

Interrogatory sentences, those that ask a question, end with a question mark.

> Did Tom invite you to his birthday party?
> What time did the pizzas arrive?

....

TIP: Beware! You should be very stingy with your exclamation marks. They can quickly lose their power if you use them too often. And a sure sign of a weak or untalented writer is one who is using exclamation points to convey meaning or emotion instead of using the words themselves to express the ideas.

....

Use periods at the end of initials and many abbreviations.

Abbreviations That Use Periods

M.D. (doctor)

Ph.D. (doctor of philosophy)

P.O. (post office)

B.A. (bachelor of arts)

P.M. (*post meridiem,* Latin for *after noon*)

A.M. (*ante meridiem,* Latin for *before noon*)

Abbreviations That Do Not Use Periods

DVD (digital video disc)

mph (miles per hour)

CIA (Central Intelligence Agency)

CA (California), NY (New York), CO (Colorado) (state designations as used by the U.S. Postal Service)

The rules for abbreviations are not entirely consistent. Your best bet is to notice carefully how certain abbreviations are being used when you read books and newspapers and websites, and memorize the accepted, standard usage.

The Ellipsis: The End Mark to Avoid

An **ellipsis** is the omission of a word or a phrase from a sentence that does not change the thought or the grammatical coherence of the sentence. The ellipsis is indicated by the use of three periods to show that something has been omitted from the sentence.

The ellipsis is best used when you are writing a research paper and quoting from another source.

Here is an example of the correct use of an ellipsis in a sentence in this lesson:

Your best bet is to notice carefully how certain abbreviations are being used . . . and memorize the accepted, standard usage.

Many writers make the mistake of using the ellipsis at the end of a sentence as a kind of trailing-off thought intended to indicate further unspecified thoughts on the part of the writer and the reader. This is a weak substitution.

....

TIP: Write what you mean; do not depend on the ellipsis to suggest something unsaid that you might have written but didn't.

....

PRACTICE 1: USING END MARKS CORRECTLY

Choose the proper end mark to use in each of the following sentences.

1. We are planning to go really crazy at our slumber party tonight

2. Do you think everyone in Topeka, Kansas, will be at the game tonight

3. The coach asked the team if they were ready to meet the enemy

4. Me It's not my fault if the secret gets out

5. Do not blame me if you get there at the wrong time

QUOTATION MARKS

Direct Quotations

Quotation marks are used to indicate that you are quoting the exact words that someone said, and you are attributing them to that person.

> Jane said, "I want to go to the game with you."
> "I will be going," said Marian, "whether or not you go."

....

TIP: Commas and periods always go inside closing quotation marks.

....

Note carefully that commas usually set off the explanatory words that accompany direct quotations. However, when an end mark is part of the direct quotation, you omit the comma:

"Do you want to come with us?" asked Marian.

"Don't you dare!" gasped his mother.

Note that the end mark (question mark or exclamation point) goes inside the quotation marks when it is part of what is being quoted. However, when the quoted words are part of a question or exclamation of your own and not the person you are quoting, the end marks go outside the quotation marks. For example:

Do I have to listen to Jane saying over and over again, "I want to go"?

I can't believe you said, "It's not a problem"!

....

TIP: If you are writing direct quotation dialogue between two people, you indicate a change in speaker by starting a new paragraph for each speaker:

"Why would you want to come with us?" said Marian. And then she smiled sweetly, hoping that Jane would not be insulted by her question.

"I think it's not a good idea for you to come," said Steve.

....

Indirect Quotations

When you restate something that someone else has said, but without using their exact words, you are using an indirect quotation. In this case, you do not use quotation marks. Here are examples of the two kinds of quotations:

Direct quotation: Jane said, "I want to go."

Indirect quotation: Jane said she wants to go.

COLONS AND SEMICOLONS

Colons are quite easy to use correctly. Use them in the following situations:

- when a list of items is to follow:

  My favorite flowers are the purple ones: pansies, irises, and violets.

- after the greeting in a formal business letter:

  Dear Dr. Jones:

  To Whom It May Concern:

- when you are describing time:

  Meet me at 7:30 A.M. for a quick breakfast before school.

Semicolons are more complicated. Use them in the following situations:

- to connect two parts of a compound sentence when you are not using a conjunction (*and, but,* and so on) to connect the two parts:

  We want to attend the game; getting there is going to be the tricky part.

- to separate parts of a list when the individual parts of the list include commas:

  The team had several problems to overcome. It had been suffering a losing streak lately; it had several injured players; and it resented its demoralized student body, which hadn't provided much support the past few months.

HYPHENS AND DASHES

Hyphens and **dashes** are used to set off specific words in your sentences. Hyphens are the more common of the two, and they appear as part of the correct spelling of many compound words. For example:

- Use a hyphen if in your typing (or writing) you must break a word in two and carry over the second part onto a second line. Use a hyphen in this way only where there is a natural syllable break.

  correct: tele-phone   *incorrect:* telepho-ne

- Use hyphens in compound words such as these:

  two-thirds   half-time   half-baked   ex-president   ex-wife

- Use dashes, which in typing and print look like long hyphens, to indicate an interruption in thought.

  The coach—who plans to retire at the end of the season—has been an inspiration for decades to all the athletes at our school.

APOSTROPHES

Apostrophes are those little commas in the air to indicate various changes in the function of the word they accompany. For example:

- Use an apostrophe to form a possessive of a singular or plural noun.

  Jane's team spirit

  the boys' team (apostrophe only; no added *s*)

  the people's votes (apostrophe and *s* when the plural noun has no final *s*)

- Use apostrophes to form contractions, but be careful not to confuse contractions and possessive pronouns.

Mixing up possessive pronouns and contractions is a common mistake, but it is easy to avoid if you stop to think and understand the difference. You use a lot of these words correctly in speech, but they often get misspelled in writing. Here's a chart to help you remember the difference between certain possessive pronouns and their cousins, the contractions.

Possessive Pronoun	Contraction
whose (whose friend)	who's (who is)
your (your friend)	you're (you are)
their (their friend)	they're (they are)
its (its head)	it's (it is)

PRACTICE 2: USING OTHER PUNCTUATION MARKS CORRECTLY

Rewrite these sentences to correct their punctuation errors, and describe briefly the error you've corrected.

1. The coach's retirement party—which isn't scheduled yet, will be sometime next week.

2. We arent going to give him any gifts, he said he didn't want any.

3. Who's parents will be the chaperones at our after game party.

4. The refreshment list includes these fruits and vegetables, apples, oranges, pineapple, carrots and celery sticks.

5. The crowds screams filled the auditorium and practically raised it's roof.

6. School ends this year on the twenty third of May, we'll have plenty of time to relax this summer.

7. Do you know whether the game starts at 8 or at 8.30?

8. I said to my parents This is the most important game of the season and I have to go to it.

9. The teams best efforts will be in evidence during this last game.

10. Because school spirit is really important to the outcome of the game we hope the team feels the spirit coming from the stand's.

ANSWERS

Practice 1: Using End Marks Correctly

1. We are planning to go really crazy at our slumber party tonight!

2. Do you think everyone in Topeka, Kansas, will be at the game tonight?

3. The coach asked the team if they were ready to meet the enemy.

4. Me? It's not my fault if the secret gets out!

5. Do not blame me if you get there at the wrong time.

Practice 2: Using Other Punctuation Marks Correctly

1. The coach's retirement party—which isn't scheduled yet—will be sometime next week.
    Incomplete use of dash

2. We aren't going to give him any gifts; he said he didn't want any.
    Apostrophe missing from contraction; missing semicolon

3. Whose parents will be the chaperones at our after-game party?
    Incorrect use of pronoun; missing hyphen; missing question mark

4. The refreshment list includes these fruits and vegetables: apples, oranges, pineapple, carrots, and celery sticks.
    Missing colon; missing series comma

5. The crowd's screams filled the auditorium and practically raised its roof.
    Plural noun should be a possessive; contraction of *it's* used instead of correct *its*

6. School ends this year on the twenty-third of May; we'll have plenty of time to relax this summer.

Hyphen needed in *twenty-third*; semicolon needed for compound sentence

7. Do you know whether the game starts at 8 or at 8:30?

Colon needed in time 8:30

8. I said to my parents, "This is the most important game of the season and I have to go to it."

Direct quotation requires introductory comma and quotation marks

9. The team's best efforts will be in evidence during this last game.

Possessive requires apostrophe

10. Because school spirit is really important to the outcome of the game, we hope the team feels the spirit coming from the stands.

Comma required after dependent introductory clause; incorrect possessive instead of plural of the word *stand*

avoiding the five most common grammatical errors

Life is tons of discipline. Your first discipline is your vocabulary,
then your grammar and your punctuation.

ROBERT FROST (1874–1963)
AMERICAN POET

This lesson gives an overview of the most common grammatical errors, and provides you with tips and reminders for avoiding these errors. Take care to read this lesson carefully, and complete its exercises thoroughly as a review and a guide to writing better prose.

THIS LESSON WILL help you learn how to avoid the most common grammatical errors. These errors are actually easy to avoid if you know the rules, and observe them.

Our review so far has provided you with an overview of the most important grammar rules, and by now you should feel more confident about your ability to write good grammatical prose. (The rules of grammar are not so strictly applied in the writing of novels, short stories, and poetry. This book assumes that you are seeking to improve your day-to-day prose writing before you go on to tackle more imaginative forms of writing.)

....

TIP: The single most useful practice you can develop as a writer is to slow down. Proofread and edit your writing very carefully, and you're certain to catch a lot of your own errors in advance of submitting your work to other readers.

....

COMMON ERROR 1: INCORRECT NOUN-VERB AGREEMENT

The Correct Rule: In every sentence you write, the noun and the verb must agree in number. This means that a singular noun must be paired with a singular verb, and a plural noun requires a plural verb.

Sounds easy, doesn't it? And yet ignoring this rule is one of the most common errors that both student and adult writers make. These errors often creep into writing during the revision process; you change a sentence around slightly, and then forget to check for noun-verb agreement in the new version. It's worth checking through your writing one more time just to look for noun-verb agreement errors.

Exceptions to the Rule

Compound subjects usually take a plural verb, but occasionally a compound subject expresses a single idea, and can take a singular verb. Here are some examples:

> War and peace is a common subject for debate in political circles.
>
> Love and marriage is the theme of many romantic movies.

Compound subjects joined by *or* and *nor* usually agree with the noun closest to that word. The use of *either/or* and *neither/nor* dictates that each of the nouns is to be treated individually as the single subject of the sentence, and therefore, a singular verb is correct. Here are some examples:

> Either a dog or a cat makes a good pet. (singular verb for singular *cat*)
>
> Either a pet or plants make good hobbies. (plural verb for plural *plants*)

PRACTICE 1: NOUN-VERB AGREEMENT

Choose the correct verb in the following sentences.

1. Singers and dancers (*make, makes*) the stage show more exciting and colorful.

2. The contestants for a place in the show (*is, are*) waiting in the lobby of the theatre.

3. Would-be performers often (*take, takes*) years to realize that they have no talent.

4. The costumes for the show (*doesn't, don't*) convey accurate information about the historical period.

5. Either a pink leotard or black tap shoes (*is, are*) required for a part in the show.

COMMON ERROR 2: INCORRECT VERB ENDINGS

Correct Verb Endings: Every verb has four basic parts that indicate the time in which the action of the verb is happening. These four parts form the building blocks with which writers and speakers can describe actions that

1. are occurring in the present
2. are occurring in an ongoing time
3. occurred at a specific time in the past
4. have or had occurred sometime in the past

All options are covered by these four parts.

Here's a chart to help you keep the four parts clearly in mind:

Sample Verbs	Present	Present Participle	Past	Past Participle
regular verb	talk	(is) talking	talked	(has) talked
irregular verb	speak	(is) speaking	spoke	(has) spoken

Note that there are two kinds of verbs: regular and irregular. For **regular verbs**, the parts are formed in similar ways, for example, by adding *ing* or *ed* to the participles, which are then accompanied by linking verbs. **Irregular verbs** do not follow standard patterns in forming their various parts. To use irregular verbs correctly, you must memorize their parts because there is no standard system for their spellings. You probably use many irregular verbs in your everyday conversations without thinking about them; you simply absorb them as you learn and use the language. However, when you write, you must pay special attention to make sure that you are using the correct form of every verb.

Here are some common irregular verbs that you should be careful to use correctly both in your speech and in your writing.

Present	Present Participle	Past	Past Participle
bring	bringing	brought	(has) brought
drink	drinking	drank	(has) drunk
shine	shining	shone	(has) shone
shrink	shrinking	shrank	(has) shrunk

COMMON ERROR 3: INCORRECT PRONOUN-ANTECEDENT AGREEMENT

Right now, before you do anything else, go back and reread the material in Lesson 3, which was all about correct pronoun use. Doing so will familiarize you with the types of pronouns that exist and refresh your memory about how to use them correctly.

Pronoun-Antecedent Agreement

The three most common errors in the use of pronouns are the following:

1. You fail to have the pronoun agree in number with its antecedent (the noun it is replacing or referring to).

   One <u>boy</u> ate <u>his</u> lunch alone. (correct agreement of singular subject and singular pronoun)

   Two <u>boys</u> ate <u>their</u> lunch alone. (correct agreement of plural subject and plural pronoun)

2. You fail to have the pronoun agree in person with its antecedent.

   Each <u>boy</u> had <u>his</u> lunch stuffed in <u>his</u> backpack. (correct agreement)

   Each <u>boy</u> had <u>their</u> lunch stuffed in <u>their</u> backpack. (incorrect agreement)

3. You fail to have the pronoun agree in grammatical function with its antecedent.

> <u>We</u> students sometimes skip lunch in order to study. (correct subjective usage)
>
> <u>Him</u> and <u>me</u> sometimes dash to Subway for lunch. (incorrect agreement: objective pronouns being used here as subjects)

Making sure that your pronouns agree with your nouns will accomplish two important goals:

1. You will help your readers keep better track of who is doing what to whom.
2. You will impress your readers as an educated, accomplished writer, instead of looking like someone who doesn't know the basics of good writing.

COMMON ERROR 4: COMMA SPLICES

As you learned in Lesson 4, no error is more common than the comma splice, and learning how to correct it is probably the single most important lesson you will learn in this review.

Here is an excerpt from Lesson 4, in which you reviewed the comma splice:

BEWARE THE COMMA SPLICE

You may have seen the term *comma splice* written by your teacher in the margins of your papers. *Comma splice* is the term used to describe the incorrect use of a comma; it is called a splice because the most common error is to splice (or slice) a sentence, dividing two independent clauses with only a comma. Beware the comma splice. It is the most common comma error, and it results from a writer's uncertainty, ignorance about comma rules, or just plain negligence.

PRACTICE 2: CORRECTING COMMA SPLICE ERRORS

Rewrite the following sentences to correct their comma splice errors.

1. Before computers typewriters were used by most students, for their assignments and personal letters.

2. After the computer, was invented, and adopted so universally, typewriters became antiques which nobody wanted.

3. Your teacher Ms. Prim demands, that you do not rely on your computer's spell check feature to correct your spelling.

4. Typing with two fingers, or using thumbs for texting is common among students who have grown up using computers.

5. Computer stores, that are very popular, attract a lot of kids who visit the mall.

COMMON ERROR 5: TEN COMMON SPELLING MISTAKES AND WORD CONFUSIONS

There are a lot of words that sound or look similar but that have very different meanings. The only way to be sure you are using these words correctly is to memorize their proper meanings.

Here is a list of ten of the most commonly misused words, with sample sentences to show you how they are used correctly.

1. Accept: verb, to take something
   Except: preposition, but, or other than

   The teacher accepted most of Tim's excuse, except the part about how the dog ate his homework.

2. Advice: noun, describes help you give someone
   Advise: verb, describes the act of giving someone verbal help

   The teacher advised the students to take her good advice and study hard for the examination.

3. Affect: verb, to modify or make a difference
   Effect: noun, a result

   > The effect of bad study habits is often seen in a student's school failures, which may affect future opportunities.

4. Bad: adjective, used with linking verbs as well as to modify nouns
   Badly: adverb, in an inferior way

   > The teacher feels bad when her students perform badly on their tests.

   > The bad result of skipping class is the failure to learn the day's lessons.

   > It is too bad that some students fail to like school.

5. Can: verb, being able to do something
   May: verb, having been given permission to do something

   > The students can study harder, but the chances that they will do so often seem slim.

   > If the students do well early in the week, the teacher may give them permission to goof off one hour on Friday.

6. Farther: adverb, describes distance
   Further: adjective, describes quantity

   > Runners who want to run farther than a mini-marathon need to invest time in further practice.

7. Lend: verb, to provide temporary use of
   Loan: noun, what you give someone temporary use of

   > Your best friend may lend you her copy of the textbook, but the loan is temporary until you find your own copy.

8. Like: preposition, introduces the idea of similarity
   As: adverb, suggests similarity, or in the same manner

   > A clap of thunder is like an alarm clock; it startles and surprises you.

   > Do as I say, not as I do. (correct usage)

   > Do like I say. (incorrect usage)

....

TIP: Try to limit your use of the word *like*. It is probably the most overused word in many vocabularies. It is not a word to introduce phrases, or to use when you can't think of what you're going to say next.

....

9. Media: noun (plural of medium), one or more means of communication or expression
   Medium: noun (singular), the use of a system of communication

   The singer's medium is hip hop, and the media have turned him into a television star.

10. Principal: as a noun, describes a manager or executive who manages a school or business department; as an adjective, describes a degree of importance
    Principle: noun, describes a rule or policy

    The principal of our school insists that we observe the principle of fair play in all our sports competitions.

    One of the principal reasons to write well is to communicate your ideas effectively.

ANSWERS

Practice 1: Noun-Verb Agreement

1. make
2. are
3. take
4. don't
5. are

Practice 2: Comma Splice Errors

1. Before computers, typewriters were used by most students for their assignments and personal letters.
2. After the computer was invented and adopted so universally, typewriters became antiques, which nobody wanted.
3. Your teacher, Ms. Prim, demands that you do not rely on your computer's spell check feature to correct your spelling.
4. Typing with two fingers or using thumbs for texting is common among students who have grown up using computers.
5. Computer stores that are very popular attract a lot of kids who visit the mall.

S E C T I O N 2

planning your essay

ALMOST ALL EXPERIENCED and professional writers agree on one thing: Sitting down and getting started is always the hardest part of writing. If you think about it, you'll realize that writing is no different from cleaning your room, doing your homework, or giving the dog a bath. You simply have to set aside some time, make some initial plans, and, most important of all, commit to getting the job done, step by step. The next four lessons provide tricks of the writing trade: techniques for brainstorming, narrowing your subject, and jumpstarting your writing. Help is on the way—starting right here.

getting started is the hardest part

*Inspiration is wonderful when it happens, but the writer
must develop an approach for the rest of the time.*
LEONARD BERNSTEIN (1918–1990)
AMERICAN COMPOSER AND CONDUCTOR

Congratulations. You've reached Lesson 7, and the grammar review is over. Now it's time to get started on the actual writing process. You won't be surprised to learn, of course, that things are not necessarily going to get simpler. Quite the contrary. Before you even set pencil to paper, or fingers to keyboard, there are several questions to answer and decisions to make.

DECIDING WHAT TO write is often more difficult than doing the actual writing. This lesson will help get you past that scary first part.

Too many writers assume that deciding what to write is the first task. Actually, defining your subject and what you will say about it is definitely *not* the first thing to do. You have several other decisions to make first, and once you've made those choices, deciding what to write should be an easier task. Here we'll review the preliminary steps you need to take before you write.

WHAT IS YOUR ASSIGNMENT?

To make things simpler, this book assumes that you are going to write a school assignment, which is usually an essay or a report of some kind. But, as you know, there are many other kinds of writing. You may be about to write a short story. Or a poem. Or an e-mail to a friend. Or a letter. Or even a diary entry.

All of these are actually writing assignments, some of which you assign to yourself. The decisions you will have to make about what and how you will write an email or a letter are just as much of an assignment as the ones you get in school. For our purposes here, we'll assume that all writing assignments require more or less the same considerations, as only short stories, novels, plays, and poetry depart seriously from the kind of writing you most often do in your school assignments.

WHO IS YOUR AUDIENCE?

Figuring out who will be reading your work is every bit as important as determining what you will say in your writing. For example, consider the following writing assignments:

- Write 500 words on the geography of Mexico.
- Write 250 words on why you deserve a scholarship to summer music camp.
- Write a 150-word thank-you note to your grandmother.
- Write a 15-word text message to your best friend.
- Write a journal entry (as long as you like) on why you are angry at your parents.

Who will be your audience (your reader or readers) for each of these assignments? Obviously, a different someone is likely to be your audience for each of these written works. If you are applying for a scholarship, you will want to address yourself to the deciding committee, and try to provide reasons to choose you that will appeal to them. On the other hand, if you're writing to your best friend, you can refer to private jokes and assume that your friend is already familiar with you and your sense of humor.

TIP: It is essential that you have a very specific idea about the identity of your audience when you finally sit down to write.

IN WHAT STYLE OR VOICE WILL YOU WRITE?

Think about how much you can tell about your classmates, or about people you see on TV, by looking carefully at the way they dress. You form an opinion about their style. The same is true about the way you write—it's called **style**. And the writing style you choose depends on two factors: your audience and your writing goal. Consider these sample possible goals you might have for a particular writing assignment:

- Your goal is to present a factual, objective report.
- Your goal is to persuade your reader of your point of view.
- Your goal is to express your gratitude for a gift or a favor.
- Your goal is to sound really smart so you'll win a prize.
- Your goal is to make a plan to meet with your reader.
- Your goal is to vent your private, personal feelings.

For each of these goals, you will want to choose a different style or tone for your writing. In general, writers use either formal or informal language to establish the tone in most writing assignments. Both are acceptable—depending on the circumstances—and sometimes even slang is fine as well.

Formal: The class completed the writing assignment promptly.

Informal: The class managed, just barely, to get the job done.

Slang: Dude, we put a dot on it!

All three sentences are acceptable, but each carries a different tone.

WHAT IS YOUR POINT OF VIEW?

A third decision you must make before you begin to write—about anything—is to decide on a point of view, which is really your opinion about the topic. One way to identify your point of view is to ask yourself, "Why am I writing this?"

Don't be a smart aleck and say "Because my teacher assigned the work!" Every single piece of writing you do has a point of view, whether you've planned it or even thought consciously about it. For example:

- Imagine that you are writing an e-mail to a friend to organize a time to go to the movies. Isn't it likely that you have an opinion about which movie you want to see and when you want to meet? In such a simple piece of writing, a point of view is being expressed, no matter how polite and flexible your invitation seems to be.

- Imagine that you are assigned a report on current environmental efforts in your community. At first glance, this seems to be an assignment calling for straightforward, objective facts. However, how do you decide which facts to include? What if you include only successful environmental programs and leave out failed efforts from the past? What if you are writing an article for the school newspaper in which you are trying to convince your readers to be more environmentally concerned? Or, on the other hand, what if you are writing a humor article for the school newspaper in which you decide to poke fun at the environmental movement. In each of these instances, your point of view will be very different. The facts you choose to include and the way you present them reveal your point of view about your subject.

As these examples illustrate, your point of view is of supreme importance in determining what you write. Be aware that you will become a more successful and accomplished writer if you think carefully and decide on a point of view before you begin writing. The decisions you make about point of view will serve as guidelines for the actual writing of your assignment.

IN WHAT GRAMMATICAL PERSON WILL YOU WRITE?

As you learned in this book's grammar review, English nouns and verbs have different forms depending on who is speaking or being spoken to or about. The various forms of these words are called **first**, **second**, or **third person**. When you are setting out to write an essay, you have to decide in which person you will write. (Often this choice is called **point of view**, which is confusing because point of view is most often a description of your opinion about a topic.)

Choosing which person to write in usually comes quite naturally, and is rarely a difficult decision to make. Usually the subject matter itself determines which grammatical person you will use. For example, if you write in the first person, your essay will likely incorporate the word *I* quite often (*I believe that practicing the piano is a waste of time*). Quite often readers will assume you are writing your own opinions and you won't need to use the word *I*, because the opinions in the essay will be assumed by the reader to be yours. In such a case, your point of view and your grammatical person are identical.

If you were to write an essay about piano practicing in the second person, it might include sentences such as *You need to practice the piano daily if you are planning to have a musical career.* Sometimes essays can be written in the second person without using the word *you*, in which case the reader understands that the audience is being addressed directly and instructed to do or believe something.

Writing in the third person is probably the most common grammatical person that writers use. Persuasive and expository essays use the third person because it provides an easy way to provide facts, opinions, and ideas. An essay titled "How to Get Ahead in the Music World" might include a third person sentence such as this: *Practicing every day and working hard at learning everything possible about music's history is probably the best way to get a head start in the music world.*

PRACTICE 1: IDENTIFYING AUDIENCE, POINT OF VIEW, AND STYLE

Imagine you are planning what to write in response to three individual class assignments. In the following chart, fill in brief descriptions of an appropriate audience, point of view, and style for each of the subjects assigned. (A sample assignment is provided.)

Assignment	Audience	Point of View	Style or Tone
movie review	I'm going to put my review on my Facebook page, so my audience is my friends and (I hope) new friends. I think I know what appeals to most kids.	I am going to say right at the top of my review that I hated the movie, and then readers will know my point of view.	I'm going to try to be funny and casual since I'm writing for other kids.
1. my school locker			
2. my best friend			
3. my future			

There are no right or wrong answers here. Your assignment is to do the necessary preplanning for imaginary assignments. Don't rush: Take your time and plan carefully. You may well be able to use the planning work you do here in subsequent lessons.

....

TIP: Be very precise in your preliminary choices for audience, point of view, and style. The more specific you are at this planning stage, the easier your work will be once you are actually writing your assignment.

....

brainstorming to discover what you think

I write entirely to find out what I'm thinking, what I'm looking at, what I see and what it means. What I want and what I fear.

JOAN DIDION (1934–)
AMERICAN NOVELIST AND ESSAYIST

Brainstorming is one of the best techniques for getting your brain (and your pen) started on an assignment. This lesson teaches you how to brainstorm effectively.

ALL WRITERS, WHETHER young students or published authors, agree on one thing: The hardest part of the whole writing process is deciding what to write. That blank page, or that flickering empty screen, can make grown men and women cry. How to begin? What to say? How to say it?

These are the questions that plague all writers as they contemplate an assignment, or even sit down to write a self-assigned diary or journal entry. This lesson introduces you to some techniques that may help you get out of that deer-in-the-headlights mood during which you're certain you'll never figure out what to write. The frustrations at the beginning of the process can often be minimized if you use some exercises to get you over the early writing hurdles.

We'll assume here that you are preparing to write an essay on a topic of your own choosing. No specific topic or details exist. Maybe you are going to write a journal entry; maybe you want to add some personality to your web page; or maybe your teacher has given you 30 minutes of free time to write whatever you like. Sounds daunting? Not if you employ some brainstorming techniques.

GROUP BRAINSTORMING

Brainstorming is a term usually employed to describe a group activity in which several people work together to come up with a solution to a problem. For an allotted time period (usually 10 to 15 minutes), members of the group throw out ideas quickly, never stopping to evaluate or criticize each other's ideas. One member may write the ideas on a whiteboard, or another may record them quickly on a piece of paper. At the end of the timed brainstorming session, the group reads over its ideas and comes up with a plan for moving forward.

PERSONAL BRAINSTORMING

You can borrow the group brainstorming strategy and do it all on your own—in your own brain—as a technique for coming up with ideas for your own unspecified writing project. Some people call this process a personal brain-storm, or a mental self-inventory. Another much simpler term for this process is listing. It is a great way to come up with writing ideas when you have no specific assigned topic. What you do during a personal brainstorming session is ask yourself a lot of questions; any of them might spark a flame and give you a perfect topic to settle on. Here are sample questions you might start with:

- What is the funniest thing that has happened to me in the past week?
- What is my favorite activity (aside from school, of course)?
- Who is the most interesting/annoying/ridiculous person I know?
- What do I like most about my best friend? My teacher? My mom?
- What gripes me the most about my little brother/sister?
- What fantasies do I have about a career when I grow up?

Note that all of these are personal questions that you can answer easily with a little thought. As soon as you find yourself hesitating at one of these questions, stay with it a while. You may have come upon a great subject for your writing project.

BRAINSTORMING ON A TOPIC

Personal brainstorming can also be an effective idea-generating technique to use when you are given a specific topic or a choice of topics to write about. Instead of choosing and then jumping immediately into writing about a topic, it is always wise to take time to think (and plan) before you begin writing. If you have a choice of topics, take five minutes and brainstorm personally about each of the topics in turn. The topic that stimulates the most ideas immediately in your brainstorming session is probably the topic you will feel most comfortable choosing.

Let's assume you have been assigned a topic that is very general, such as global warming. Most large topics like this are completely open ended. The topic itself does not direct you to a way of writing about it.

FIRST STEPS IN BRAINSTORMING

Here are the essential first steps you might take to begin your brainstorming about the topic; jot down your thoughts about these first steps and keep them in front of you as reminders of decisions you've made.

- Establish your audience clearly in your mind. Are you writing a school essay, an editorial for the school newspaper, a letter to your congressperson? As you learned is the previous lesson, identifying your reader is the first step in any writing project.
- Once you've identified your audience, it is usually possible to settle on a writing style. These two are usually fairly connected. You wouldn't want to joke around in a school assignment, but you might well want to crack some jokes in the school newspaper.
- Identifying your point of view is definitely not possible at this point. Instead, you need to narrow the topic dramatically. Global warming is far too broad a topic to write about in general terms. You need to focus your thoughts.

HOW TO BRAINSTORM EFFECTIVELY

- Establish a time limit for yourself. Depending on the amount of time you have to write (30 minutes of a timed assignment or one week for a school assignment, and so on), your brainstorming session might be as short as five minutes or as long as 30 minutes one day and another 30 minutes a day later, once you've had time for your ideas to simmer overnight.

- Write down ideas, without editing or polishing them, as quickly as you can. Jot down whatever comes to you—individual words, phrases, questions—and don't worry about their making sense or appearing in order.

- Once your time is up, take a deep breath, and try to clear your brain. If you have time, get up and jog in place for five minutes to activate your energy.

- Now look over the ideas you've brainstormed and evaluate them. Cross out the ideas that strike you as unworkable; underline the ideas and/or words that strike a chord in your brain. Add to the brainstorming list if related or additional ideas come to you.

- Somewhere within your jottings you have undoubtedly written something about the subject that appeals to you as a topic for your essay. Spend another few minutes brainstorming about the topic you've chosen. This further brainstorming will undoubtedly refine your topic further and reveal your point of view about the topic.

SAMPLE PERSONAL BRAINSTORM ON A TOPIC

Here's a sample of one student's personal brainstorm on the topic of global warming. Note that personal brainstorming can include questions as well as more fully formed ideas about a topic. The questions are often the most useful jottings in a personal brainstorm; they trigger ideas for specific topics.

This student ultimately decided to write an essay about the effect of global warming on polar bears. Can you think of other topics the student might have settled on, given the personal brainstorming she did? She might have chosen to write a more personal essay, for example, by choosing to use her father's experiences at his favorite fishing spot as the starting point for an essay about local effects of global patterns. Or she might have chosen to write about the effects of global warming on a particular country; her mention of Peru suggests that she has some interest in or information about that country.

Do you see how useful personal brainstorming can be in helping you narrow your focus and find a topic for an essay? There are no rights or wrongs in brainstorming. The intent of the exercise is to get your mind juiced up and working.

MY GLOBAL WARMING BRAINSTORMING IDEAS

Big issue in politics—is it Democrats or Republicans who will fix it more?

Future generations will suffer. How fast is it happening?

Polar bears are dying out because of ice caps melting

What about other animals? seals, sharks, dolphins?

Fumes from cars are causing earth to heat up

Factories—are they the cause of it? What about little countries like Peru?

How much is due to China being so important nowadays?

Last summer was hottest summer we've had—even my uncle's corn crop got ruined

Atmosphere has a hole in it. (I don't really know what this means)

My dad's complaint about his fishing being affected . . . no more salmon in the river

Define global anyway. What does it really mean? Is the weather only world feature changing? Is the soil drying up? What about the oceans?

PRACTICE 1: PRACTICING PERSONAL BRAINSTORMING

On a separate piece of paper (or on your computer), take five minutes and do a personal brainstorm for an essay on one of these topics. After you have completed your brainstorm, write out the topic, its audience, point of view, and style for your imagined essay.

1. Television is probably the most powerful medium in the world today.

2. Social activities are as important to students as their studies.

3. Are computers useful as teaching devices in schools?

9

mapping your subject

Writing is like walking in a deserted street.
Out of the dust in the street you make a mud pie.

JOHN LE CARRÉ (1931–)
BRITISH SPY NOVELIST

This lesson introduces techniques for organizing your thoughts and beginning the preliminary work of planning your essay.

IN THE CONSTANT search to find ways to make their writing easier, writers use various techniques to help organize their thoughts and plan their work. One of the simplest devices used for planning is called a **cluster diagram**, or a **concept map**. (The names are really interchangeable, so use whichever one makes more sense to you.)

Concept maps can be very useful brainstorming tools. If you tend to think in pictures, you may find that jotting down your ideas during the planning stage in map form is a helpful way both to get your ideas down on paper and to visualize the relationships between various ideas. Here is a sample concept map created by a student planning an essay on how sports influence popular culture.

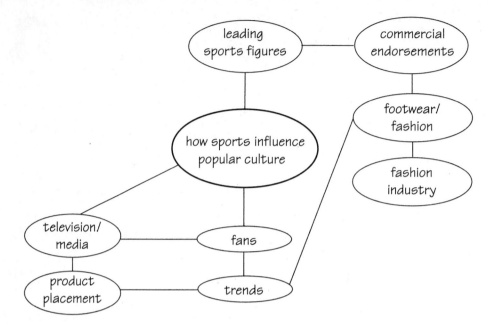

HOW TO CREATE A CONCEPT MAP

There is no right and wrong way to create a concept map, and it is important that you do not censor yourself when you're drawing the map. Write down your ideas in any order, and draw circles (or ovals or stars) around them to keep them separated from one another. And then sit back and consider them. See if you can see relationships among the ideas, and if you do, connect them with lines or arrows. You may want to cross out some of your ideas that don't contribute to the logic or map of the topic that has emerged during the drawing of the concept map.

Following you'll see a concept map drawn by a student doing the preplanning for an essay about environmental issues in his town. Note that he has been very careful to try to create the map in a very orderly fashion, with ideas radiating in a prioritized manner—big ideas lead down to smaller ideas.

You may not think in such an orderly way and your maps might not look so tidy, which is perfectly all right. What's important is to get lots of ideas down on paper so that you can reorganize your ideas into a different order once you sit down to write the draft of your essay.

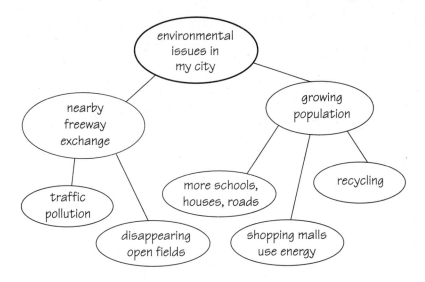

CREATING A MIND MAP

A similar tool that many writers find useful is called a **mind map**. To create a mind map, the writer starts from a central idea, drawn usually in a circle in the center of the map, and related ideas are generated in circles radiating out from the central idea. Writers who prefer mind maps to concept maps emphasize that the mind map allows them to think randomly, without having to create big ideas that generate smaller ideas below them. Using a mind map, the writer visualizes all of his ideas as being of equal weight; subsequent planning will then, of course, require that ideas be reorganized into generalizations and specifics. Here is an example of the mind map that the student who planned to write about environmental issues might have created.

PRACTICE 1: CREATING YOUR OWN MIND MAP

In Lesson 7, you completed an exercise that asked you to identify an audience, a point of view, and a style for an essay about your school locker. Now, imagine that you are at the next stage of the essay assignment.

On a separate piece of paper, create a mind map for the essay on your school locker. Start with the words *school locker* in a center circle. Spend just three minutes (use a kitchen timer!) creating ideas for this essay.

Remember, there are no right and wrong answers. This exercise will help you understand how useful mind maps can be in helping you plan any and all kinds of writing assignments.

PRACTICE 2: CREATING YOUR OWN CONCEPT MAP

Now take another three minutes and draw a concept map for an essay assignment that asks "What Will Your Future Be?"

Remember that concept maps usually visualize ideas in a prioritized pattern or format (general ideas → specific examples), but you are not required to draw your maps in any prescribed way. This exercise will help you know which kind of map feels right to you.

Are you a mind map person or a concept map/cluster diagram person? Think about why you prefer one technique over the other. Perhaps you'll want to take these assignments to school and discuss them with your classmates and teachers. Your teachers might be delighted to have you plan a lesson for the class!

how to jumpstart your writing

True ease in writing comes from art, not chance,
As those move easiest who have learn'd to dance.
ALEXANDER POPE (1688–1744)
ENGLISH POET

This lesson teaches you how to do freewriting, a highly effective way of getting started on your assignments. This lesson provides another technique experienced writers use to help them jumpstart the writing process. Don't for a minute think that you are alone, as a young writer, in fearing the blank page. Every writer encounters the same preliminary fears, and every writer uses whatever tricks are available to get over the hurdle and into the writing task at hand.

WRITING ISN'T QUITE as challenging or nearly as dangerous as climbing Mount Everest; it only feels that way. And just as serious climbers have to train on smaller mountains, writers often warm up by doing practice writing sessions, called *freewriting*.

DEFINING FREEWRITING

Freewriting is the practice of writing continuously (usually in a timed session of about five or ten minutes), without delays to correct spelling, grammar, or sentence structure. If you get stuck and can't think of anything more to write, then you write about that ("I am stuck and can't think of anything else to write . . . and then oh, I thought of how I feel about. . . ."). Actually, freewriting can be understood as the written form of idle thinking, the kind of mind wandering you do when you're on the bus, or waiting to fall asleep, or trying not to pay attention to the boring conversation of the adults in the room.

In freewriting, you don't worry about staying on topic. Many find that it's easier to begin their freewriting with a topic, no matter how simple or vague, and then to let their writing take them anywhere. Once you're started writing, you let your mind (and your fingers) do the choosing. There is often an advantage to beginning your freewriting session with a certain focused topic. You may find yourself coming up with connections and ideas you wouldn't have come to had you been using some other planning technique before beginning a writing assignment.

....

TIP: If you don't already know how to touch type, which means typing quickly without looking at the keys, learn how! Touch typing is every writer's favorite skill. Being able to type quickly will make your writing better, because you won't lose your train of thought while you're hunting and pecking, and revising your work is much easier when you aren't fumbling around.

Ask your parents to buy a learn-to-type software program, with which you can teach yourself touch typing on the computer, or enroll in a typing class at school. Touch typing is not only a skill that you'll be grateful for your whole life, but it's also fun—it's like being able to sing and ride your bike at the same time.

....

Here's a sample of freewriting done by a student preparing to write a school essay about *The Influence of Television on My Life*. Note that the freewriting veers off the subject occasionally, but that the student manages to come up with several ideas that might be reorganized into specific examples and relevant points for the finished essay.

Does freewriting appeal to you more as a useful technique now that you see a sample of it?

I am really stuck trying to think of what to write about this topic, because television is a really important part of everybody life. Think of the war, we see it everyday on tv and then there are elections and politics and the goverrrment and the topic seems so big that I think the teacher wants to bad mouth television because she is always trying to get us to read books instead of watching tv so I thitkn this assignment is mostly to get us to say that we watch too mcuh television. The influence of television is really great, that's for sure. Think of how we get out news I don't read the papers and my parents don't even subscribe to a newspaper because when they did the papers would just pile up and no one had time in busy lifes to sit down and read all that detailed stuff that was not so important really and that is another reason that tv is very important because it becomes a way for all of us to learn things that we wouldn't kno if we dindt watch tv. And theirs also the entertainment factor. Plus babysitting. When I was little me and my brother watchd sesame street and I can remember even lerning stuff from that show that I still know. So maybe what I should write about is all the good things from tv and not try to suck up to the teacher and say that ttv is bad for us cause I think that is what she wants to hear in this paper.

WHAT IS PREWRITING?

Some writers refer to the technique of freewriting as *prewriting* because they do it every day as a routine preparation for their day's writing work. Technically, prewriting is more focused on a specific topic. It can be defined as the very first, before-the-first-draft, writing that you do for an assignment. The freewriting student sample above might well be identified by many as prewriting because it was written in response to a specific assignment. Whether you use the term *prewriting* or *freewriting*, you're doing approximately the same thing. It's like stretching before a run, or throwing a few pitches before the game begins.

KEEPING A DIARY OR A JOURNAL

Many writers, and many students who have not yet begun to identify themselves as writers, keep a diary or a journal. In fact, the practice of keeping a journal has now become a verb: *to journal.* Journaling does not have to be a daily practice, but many people find that writing a little (or a lot) every day helps them in numerous ways.

- Journaling provides a place to record private thoughts that the writer doesn't feel comfortable sharing with others.
- Journaling is often prescribed by doctors who find that writing helps people get through physical or emotional problems they are experiencing.
- Journaling is a good way to vent. Better to yell at someone in your private journal than to yell at them in person.
- Journaling helps writers improve their craft. "Practice makes perfect," just as your mother may have told you.
- Journaling provides a good place for warehousing an inventory of ideas you'd like to write about someday. This is perhaps the most common writer's use of journaling. Ideas for future poems, stories, and essays can be recorded in the journal and kept there for future reference and development.

WHAT ABOUT BLOGS?

A blog is a relatively recent invention that originated on the Internet. The word *blog* is what's called a portmanteau word. (*Portmanteau* is a French word for *suitcase*; in this context, a portmanteau is a word that fuses two words into a new word with its own meaning.) The portmanteau word *blog* is created by combining web and log. Thus, a blog is actually an online diary or journal.

Blogs consist of short Internet posts on a single topic (for example, politics, music, sports, and so on), and they usually contain links to other blogs or web pages. Some blogs are strictly personal, and constitute a private journal that the writer is willing for the world to read. Many blogs allow readers to comment interactively.

The blog format allows the writer to write more or less informally, because blog entries are not expected to be formal essays on a specific topic. Instead, the writer is putting his or her immediate thoughts out on the Internet and inviting readers to join the conversation. While blogs are not technically identical to freewriting, they often read that way because of their immediacy. Interestingly, some television commentators are now blogging while they are on the air, and inviting viewers to interact via the Internet while simultaneously watching the television show. Have any of your favorite shows done this yet? Voting for *American Idol* doesn't count, although it is a related type of simultaneous interaction with a television broadcast.

Researchers estimate that there are more than 150 million blogs currently on the Internet. Do you read (or write) any of them?

PRACTICE 1: FREEWRITING EXERCISE

Now try freewriting on your own. Set your kitchen timer for three minutes and do freewriting on the topic *Learning How to Write Better*. See what you come up with.

You may write here, on a separate piece of paper, or on your computer. Choose the place that will encourage you to write most freely.

SECTION 3

defining your topic and thesis

FOR MOST WRITERS approaching a writing project, the real problem is deciding what to say about the assigned (or chosen) topic. Even when you are invited to choose your own topic, it's often frustrating to figure out how to attack your subject. The next three lessons will show you how to develop a topic, and then how to define your thesis, which is really the summary statement of what you want to say about your topic. Once you've defined your thesis, you'll be more than halfway toward getting ready to write.

techniques for defining and developing a topic

*If any man wish to write in a clear style, let him
be first clear in his thoughts; and if any would write
in a noble style, let him first possess a noble soul.*

JOHANN WOLFGANG VON GOETHE (1749–1832)
GERMAN POET, DRAMATIST, AND NOVELIST

This lesson reviews techniques for how to develop your topic. Whether or not you've been assigned a specific topic, you'll need to do some defining and refining work. You'll also learn here how to use the 5 Ws.

BY NOW YOU'VE read about and practiced several techniques to help you prepare to write:

- establishing your audience, point of view, and style
- brainstorming
- concept mapping (or cluster diagramming)
- freewriting
- journaling

Now it's time to tackle the problem of what to write. And the first step in that process is defining your topic. In most classroom situations, your teacher will have assigned a topic, but in the great majority of those cases, the assigned topic is so general and open-ended that you will be required to do significant narrowing and focusing before you can begin to write your essay.

Similarly, once you go on to other levels of schooling (high school, college, even graduate work), you will face the same task: Writing assignments purposely leave room for students to maneuver within them. One of the ways in which you are judged by your teachers is the skill with which you identify a particular angle to use in responding to the assignment. And the same is true for people out in the working world. Someday your boss may ask you to write up a memo or a report on some subject, and you will need to go through exactly the same steps of narrowing and focusing the topic that you are learning here. So sit up and pay attention. This is important information that will be useful to you for the rest of your life.

DEVELOPING A TOPIC

Once you've done your freewriting, and identified your audience, your style, and your point of view, you must begin the development of your topic. Let's assume that you've been given the following assignment:

"Write an essay about environmental issues in your community."

That's the whole assignment; no specifics or particulars are offered. Where to begin?

You may want to begin the development of your topic by taking a step backward and doing some freewriting on the general topic. You may find that an idea for a topic emerges during the freewriting process. However, freewriting is most often an effective strategy when you already have an assigned topic or at least a general idea of what you will be writing about. So for most writers, the process of developing a topic requires taking the following steps.

Create some categories of information about the general subject and ask yourself as many questions as you can think of that pertain to each subcategory you've created:

- questions that focus on recycling:
  — Is there a recycling program in the town?
  — Does my school practice recycling?
  — Does my family practice recycling?
  — Should businesses continue to be fined if they don't recycle?
  — Is recycling really helping the environment or is it just a Band-Aid?

- questions that focus on energy use:
  — What effect does the airport have on the atmosphere?
  — Should cars with only one passenger be banned from the freeways?
  — Is the factory outside of town creating air pollution?
- questions that focus on the future:
  — How is global warming affecting the town's daily life?
  — Are weather patterns actually changing or does it just seem so?
  — Do air pollutants cause cancer?

Jotting down questions such as these will help you discover a hook, an approach to the huge subject of environmental issues that enables you to define a workable topic for your essay.

Taking time to list these questions, even if you have been allotted only a certain amount of time to write the essay, is essential. The questions will focus your thinking and help you avoid the common trap of starting to write without a clear topic in mind.

ASK THE 5 Ws

Another technique for developing a topic is to imagine that you are a reporter or a detective investigating the subject. Think about your favorite cop show on TV. How do the police go about investigating crimes? Or pick up any newspaper and analyze one or two stories carefully; near the beginning of any article, whether it's short or long, you will find the answers to the 5 W questions:

who?

what?

where?

when?

why?

PRACTICE 1: ASKING THE 5 Ws

On a separate piece of paper, take three minutes and write out some 5 W questions prompted by the assignment to write about environmental issues in your community.

You may find yourself writing as many as ten W questions, or even more; they should keep popping into your mind. Just begin each question with one of the W words.

Once you've asked your 5 W questions, write out a possible essay topic that emerges from one or more of these W questions.

USING THE 5 W QUESTIONS TO NARROW A TOPIC

Let's assume that one of the questions you wrote down was the following:

Who is doing the most to promote recycling?

That one question alone could be the topic of a whole essay, once you know the answer to your question.

Here's another question you might have asked:

Which kind of recycling is more useful—bottles or cans?

At first glance, that question might seem too narrow to support a whole essay, but in fact, it could easily become the topic for your essay once you have taken the next step in developing a topic: research.

DOING YOUR RESEARCH

If you are sitting in class and your teacher has given you 30 minutes to write an essay, of course you don't have time to do any outside research. But in most other cases, you are assigned an essay and given plenty of time to do some research.

Research can be a scary word, but all it really means is "gather some facts, opinions, and quotations from interested parties or authorities, and other items that provide the evidence you need to support your thesis statement." (We'll discuss developing your thesis in the next lesson.)

WHAT KIND OF RESEARCH WORKS BEST?

Clever, imaginative, thoughtful research is what you should aim for. Your essay will improve in exact proportion to the quality of research that you do. Books, magazines, newspapers, and interviews are the obvious places to start. But you'll need to do a lot of narrowing before your research will start producing helpful results. For example, a search on Google for *environmental issues* produces 18,000,000 pages!

Just as narrowing your topic is essential to the development of a workable essay topic, research must be very carefully focused if it is to provide information and specific data to support your thesis. Your preliminary research will need to be very general of course. In the beginning, when you are deciding on a topic, you will be looking at the larger picture. Once you have decided on a topic, you will then be able to zoom in and focus your research on the specifics of the topic you have chosen.

Tips on Creative Research

- If you need help doing the research for your essay, go to your local library and ask for help. Librarians love to help people learn how to use a library.
- Try to organize an interview with at least one authority on your subject. This doesn't mean you need to get to your senator. You might want to interview the principal of your school, or the person in the mayor's office who oversees your city's recycling program. Get on the phone and ask—someone will say yes if you make a good case for why you want to meet the authority and how your interview will benefit the authority and you.
- Think creatively. If you have decided to write, for example, a comparison of the effectiveness of recycling bottles versus cans, why not try to interview the manager of the local soft drink distributor. He may have helpful information to offer.
- Provide your own data. If you don't have time to arrange interviews, and you can't find data easily to support your thesis, conduct your own small experiment. Weigh some bottles and cans, go to the local recycling center, and see what happens when you try to recycle your materials. You won't be solving the world's recycling problems, but you will have demonstrated how complicated the problems are that need solving.

PRACTICE 2: DOING CREATIVE RESEARCH

Imagine that you have decided to write an essay based on your question, *Who is doing the most to promote recycling?*

Take five minutes and create a minimum of three creative ideas for research on this topic.

In the next lesson, we'll explore ways to develop and refine your essay's thesis statement.

LESSON 12

finding and developing a thesis

Say all you have to say in the fewest possible words,
or your reader will be sure to skip them, and in the plainest
possible words or he will certainly misunderstand them.

JOHN RUSKIN (1819–1900)
ENGLISH POET AND ESSAYIST

This lesson takes you to the next step in the planning process: deciding on a thesis statement for your essay. Knowing in advance what you're going to say about your topic is essential to good writing.

IN THE PREVIOUS lesson, you learned about how to develop a topic for an essay. In this lesson, you'll learn how to develop and refine your essay's thesis. The distinction between a topic and a thesis is extremely important. Make sure you understand how they differ:

topic: the subject matter, the data or situation that you are writing about, in your magazine article, essay, book, or whatever

thesis: the position you are taking about the topic

A **thesis statement** presents the idea or argument that you intend to support in your essay.

The last lesson introduced the question *Who is doing the most to promote recycling?* Had that been a real essay assignment, and had you done research and thinking about the topic, you would have been ready to develop a thesis statement for your essay. Here are some possible thesis statements for this topic:

1. Nonprofit community activist groups in the city are doing the most to promote recycling.
2. The city government is leading the drive to promote recycling.
3. The city government, the city schools, and local church groups are equally active in promoting recycling.
4. The recycling activity in the city is practically invisible—nobody is doing very much to promote this important activity.

Note that each of these sentences states in very few words the idea you will be exploring in the proposed essay. Be sure to distill your thesis statement into as few words as possible so that you can keep clearly in your mind (and in the mind of the reader) the most basic point that you are trying to make in your essay.

HOW TO DEVELOP A THESIS

As you are well aware, one of the trickiest part about writing is deciding what to write. And within the general area of planning, probably the toughest part of all is pinpointing your thesis. You may have done lots of reading, thinking, and researching, and still not know exactly what it is you want to say in your essay. Here are some guidelines to help you distill your thinking and identify a thesis for your essay.

STEP 1: MAKE YOUR THESIS INTERESTING

Make sure your thesis is interesting, both to you and to your potential readers. If you're not interested by the thesis you are considering, it will show in your writing, and you can be pretty sure your readers won't be interested either.

A good way to ensure that your thesis has interest value is to give it a little twist or controversy or shock. Look at the four sample thesis statements from the recycling example. Which one is most interesting? Which essay do you think you'd want to read? Probably you'll say number 4, because it has a bit of spice and surprise. It makes the reader wonder how the writer will prove this statement to be true about the city.

STEP 2: KEEP YOUR THESIS STATEMENT FOCUSED

Most essay topics that you are assigned are quite broad. They might be topics such as *What is your favorite movie?* or *What is your career goal?* or *Who has influenced you the most?* Or a teacher might ask you to write an essay about a book your class has read, or a news event that interests you.

All of these topics are very general, and may not immediately grab your attention or the interest of your reader. Your job as a writer is to establish a thesis statement for your essay that is very specific and narrow, and communicates your point of view about the topic. For example, in response to the assignment to write about your favorite book, you might decide on a thesis statement such as one of these:

1. My favorite book is _____ because it opened my eyes to the importance of _____ .
2. My favorite book is my own diary because in it I write _____ .
3. I haven't yet found a favorite book because _____ .

Do you see how these thesis statements narrow the topic, establish a point of view or an argument to be supported in the essay? Which do you think is most interesting? Which essay do you want to read? Why?

STEP 3: MEET THE ASSIGNMENT'S REQUIREMENTS EXACTLY

A frequent mistake that writers make is to stray away from the assignment. In some cases, this won't matter. But most of the time, when you are taking a test, entering a contest, or writing an application for a scholarship of some kind, it is essential that you pay close attention to the essay assignment and fulfill its requirements.

Paying close attention to the assignment can also help you plan your essay more easily. Read the assignment carefully, and once you've established your thesis statement, go back and reread the assignment to make sure you're meeting its requirements. For example, many assignments ask you to support your argument with a certain number of facts or reasons; other assignments might ask you to avoid stating personal opinions. Whatever the assignment, it is your obligation as a careful (and smart) writer to read the rules carefully and obey them.

Often the requirement that gets ignored, or forgotten, is the length requirement. When an assignment calls for 300 words, it usually means that exactly, and you may well be penalized if your essay is significantly shorter or longer than the stipulated length. In general, if you come within 25–50 words either way of the required length, you'll be safe. No reader is likely to count as carefully as you do, but you definitely should be aware of length requirements and how closely you are meeting them.

....

TIP: The professional way to count words does not count every individual word equally; little words like *a*, *an*, and *the* do not count as whole words. Instead, most official word counts figure that approximately four to five characters constitute a word. Thus, to be absolutely precise, you count the number of characters in a line (including spaces), and then count the number of lines in your document, and that gives you the official word count. If you are writing on a computer, choose to use its word count tool, and note that the computer's program is probably counting in the official way.

....

STEP 4: DOUBLE-CHECK YOUR THESIS BEFORE YOU WRITE

Before you begin the actual drafting of your essay, reread the assignment and double-check your thesis statement to assure yourself that you are responding directly and precisely to the assignment. Check to see that you have developed a thesis that both states a point of view and is sufficiently focused to serve as the guiding statement throughout your essay.

PRACTICE 1: DEVELOPING THESIS STATEMENTS

Take five minutes and develop three possible thesis statements for each of these essay topics. Remember to write a narrow statement that presents a point of view and directly addresses the assigned topic. Be sure to follow the four steps outlined in this lesson as you develop your thesis statements.

1. Write an essay about coeducation in middle schools in America.

2. Write an essay about the use of school uniforms in middle schools in America.

getting ready to write

Have common sense and stick to the point.
W. SOMERSET MAUGHAM (1874–1965)
ENGLISH NOVELIST

In this lesson, you will learn how to save yourself time in the end. By reevaluating your thesis statement and doing preliminary planning, you'll be able to cut down on your actual writing time.

THIS LESSON WILL guide you through the preliminary steps you need to take before you actually begin to write your essay. All this preparation may seem tedious and boring, but you will benefit in the end. Writing your essay becomes a much less painful process if you've prepared adequately in advance.

STEP 1: REEVALUATE YOUR THESIS STATEMENT

Sometimes in the rush to get started on an essay, you get impatient, throw up your hands, and decide you've simply got to get started writing. And so you begin prematurely, before you've had time to reconsider and reevaluate your thesis statement.

Don't rush into writing. It's always a good idea to take a break, walk around the house, or even sleep on it, and then come back to take a hard last look at the statement that is going to be the cornerstone of everything you write in your assignment.

CHECKLIST FOR THESIS STATEMENT DEVELOPMENT

A good thesis statement:	A weak thesis statement is:
explains your subject clearly	an incomplete thought or fragment
clarifies your point of view	a simple statement of fact
justifies your reason for writing	a vague personal opinion
supports itself with facts or other evidence or examples	an unsupported declaration
presents material in a lively, interesting way	a simple assertion of information with no particular zing or spice
A Sample Good Thesis:	**A Sample Weak Thesis:**
Important studies show that kids today are watching too much television.	I will show in this essay that kids are watching too much television.

Once you've reevaluated your thesis statement, and perhaps revised it in light of the checklist here, it's time to start thinking about how to organize your essay. In later lessons, we'll look in detail at the various types of essay organization; for right now, it's important to think in very general terms about the structure of your essay.

STEP 2: IMAGINE THE THREE PARTS OF AN ESSAY

Every essay, no matter what is its length, subject matter, or organizational pattern, is made up of three parts:

1. introduction
2. body
3. conclusion

Think of yourself as a bird flying over the landscape and looking down. View your essay from on high, and contemplate its borders, its hills and valleys, from above. If you think in these lofty terms right at the beginning, you're likely to be able to swoop down more easily later in the writing process to look at details up close and personal.

THE INTRODUCTION OF THE ESSAY

The introduction of the essay typically includes the thesis statement. However, the thesis statement does not have to appear as the first sentence. In certain cases, you can write a whole introductory paragraph that does not include the thesis statement at all. In such an instance, it is probably best to put the thesis statement near the top of the second paragraph so that the reader doesn't get confused trying to figure out what the essay is really about. Here's an example:

> I walked into the interview not knowing what to expect, but confident that I had come prepared with a list of challenging questions for the principal. She looked at me sternly, and nodded for me to take a seat. Feeling a bit jittery, I stumbled as I sat down, and giggled nervously. But I took a deep breath, regained my calm, and decided to plunge right in.
>
> "I'm here to represent all the students in the eighth grade," I explained, "and we are prepared to boycott classes if you institute a rule requiring us to wear school uniforms." All the kids in my class had voted, and we wanted the principal to know just how seriously we were opposed to the proposal that we wear school uniforms.

Note that the reader has to wait until the second paragraph to find out what the essay is about, but note also how interested you as a reader are by the drama created in the first paragraph. This is good writing, and good use of delaying the thesis of the essay.

There are numerous ways to introduce an essay, so don't fall into the same old trap of starting out with a direct statement of your thesis. Spark up your introduction in any way you can.

Tips on Writing an Interesting Introduction

- Ask a question, whether or not you answer it right away.
- Use a quotation, which needn't be from a famous person; it might come from someone you've interviewed for the essay.
- Include a startling or shocking fact that will grab your reader's attention.

- Include a dramatic description of a situation or event related to your topic.
- Start out with an exclamation: "Wow . . . who knew the problem was this great!" This isn't a question that calls for an answer; it's simply a dramatic device (known as a **rhetorical question**) that can often be used effectively. Be cautious about using this device; it is quite informal and may not be appropriate in many assigned essays.

THE BODY OF THE ESSAY

Wherever you decide to put your thesis statement, make sure that every subsequent paragraph supports your thesis statement. This is absolutely essential to a well-written essay. The body paragraphs, no matter how many of them there are, must build on—and ideally, expand on—the idea put forth in the thesis statement.

It is helpful to think of your essay as a puzzle. Each piece contributes to the whole, and the picture wouldn't be complete without all those little parts. Alternatively, think of each paragraph as a steppingstone in a path that leads to your final conclusion. But be careful: Don't let your path take too many detours and wind around unnecessarily. The path should be straight as an arrow—each paragraph following the one before, either elaborating on or supporting it, or adding new information that builds toward the conclusion.

THE CONCLUSION OF THE ESSAY

Weak conclusions simply repeat the thesis statement from the introduction:

In conclusion, it is clear that kids are watching too much television.

Strong conclusions offer a summation of the thesis statement and offer either some new insight, or at the very least something more to think about.

> While the most reputable studies are unanimous in their condemnation of the amount of time most middle school students spend watching television, there is strong evidence that the Internet is replacing television as a favorite pastime for kids aged 8 to 12. Does this mean that kids are learning something useful while they're staring at their computer screens? Let's hope so.

PRACTICE 1: EVALUATING THESIS STATEMENTS

Fill in the following chart with improved thesis statements to replace the weak thesis statements provided. Please note the sample response provided. If you need more room, use a separate piece of paper. Save your answers; they will be useful in subsequent lessons.

Weak Thesis Statement	Strong Thesis Statement
Video games are very popular.	Video games are stealing time away from homework for many middle school kids in our community.
Sports play a part in school life.	
Kids watch television a lot.	
Parents nag their kids too much about homework.	

PRACTICE 2: WRITING LIVELY INTRODUCTIONS

For the three strong thesis statements that you have written, write an opening sentence, or complete introductory paragraph, for the essays that might follow your thesis statements.

If you like, you may write your introductory sentences (or paragraphs) right in this chart. If you do so, they'll be easy to refer back to during subsequent lessons. Otherwise, write them on a separate piece of paper and be sure to save what you've written for future use.

Thesis Statement	Introductory Sentence or Paragraph
Video games are stealing time away from homework for many middle school kids in our community.	A survey conducted in 2007 among middle school students in the state of California revealed that 38% of students use "a significant portion of their homework time" playing video games.

SECTION 4

organizing your essay

EVERY TASK NEEDS a plan—no matter how simple it is. Think of what you do every morning to get ready for your day. How many steps are involved? Do you do them more or less in the same order every day? Why do you do them in the order you've chosen? These are the very questions every writer must ask, and answer, before beginning to write. The next four lessons provide guidance on the tricky (and sometimes scary) subjects of outlining and organizing your writing. Plus you'll learn tips for figuring out how to write effective responses to assigned topics.

before you write, organize and outline

I always write a good first line, but I have trouble in writing the others.

MOLIÈRE (1622–1673)
FRENCH PLAYWRIGHT

This lesson will teach why writing an outline is one of the smartest preparatory things you can do as a writer. In the previous lesson, you learned about the three principal parts of every essay (introduction, body, and conclusion). Now we'll explore the subject of organizing an essay in more detail.

THE MOST COMMON organizational tool that writers use is the outline—either in rough form or in a formal, detailed format. Stay calm now. The idea of writing an outline may scare you, but relax. This lesson is going to make the process of writing an outline very easy.

WHY WRITE AN OUTLINE?

While writing an outline may seem like extra work—and hard work at that—the benefits of writing an outline are numerous:

- An outline provides a path for you to follow once you are immersed in the drafting process.
- An outline will let you know if your thesis is workable or weak. Your thesis may be too broad or too narrow, or it may not be making a

strong enough assertion to support an entire essay. Whatever the weakness, it's likely to show up during the outlining process.

- An outline will alert you to weak areas in your argument; it will provide signals that you need to do more research or that you don't have enough support for your thesis.

- An outline will relieve a lot of your nervousness and anxiety about writing. You'll know ahead of time how your essay is going to develop, so you'll be less likely to experience writer's block, which is the paralysis that writers describe when they get stuck and don't know what to write next.

WRITING AN INFORMAL OUTLINE

The simplest outline format is merely a quick summary of what you plan to put in each paragraph. Here's a sample informal outline:

Title: Should School Uniforms Be a Requirement in Our School?

Introduction: Thesis Statement
School uniforms should be instituted in our school because they will relieve tensions among students and make all students feel equal.

Body of Essay
Paragraph 1: statement of thesis and description of controversy throughout the country
Paragraph 2: list of reasons why school uniforms are a good idea
Paragraph 3: description of the high costs of school uniforms
Paragraph 4: description of negative reactions among some students
Paragraph 5: quotation and comments from a principal that has rejected the use of uniforms

Conclusion
While there has been some serious criticism within the student body about the use of school uniforms, there is good evidence that uniforms do create a more democratic atmosphere and reduce tensions among students. An experiment for a year to try out the use of uniforms seems to be an ideal solution to the controversy.

WRITING A FORMAL OUTLINE

Formal outlines are much more detailed; they include a lot of specific information about particular points that will be made and the supporting arguments that will be offered. A formal outline therefore provides a helpful guide to the writer as the essay progresses. Here is part of the formal outline that might be written for an essay on school uniforms.

I. Introduction
   A. Thesis statement
   B. Description of issue as it exists in our school
II. National controversy about uniforms
   A. Summary of statistics available about use of uniforms throughout U.S.
      1. Interview with a principal who has added uniforms
      2. Excerpt from a national study on use of uniforms
   B. Proponents of school uniforms
      1. church-affiliated school
      2. private prep schools
      3. residential, disciplinary schools
      4. interview with member of local school board
   C. Opponents of school uniforms
      1. National statistics showing they don't help resolve tensions
      2. Interview with a local school board member opposed to uniforms
III. Local reactions to the controversy
   A. Students and others who support the idea of uniforms
      1. Interview with student body president
      2. Interview with members of Parents' Organization
   B. Students and others opposed to the idea of uniforms
      1. Interview with the student leading the protest against uniforms
IV. Cost analysis of the use of uniforms
   A. Costs to order uniforms
      1. Interview with department store executive about uniform costs and delivery details
      2. compare to costs of sports uniforms
   B. Options for helping disadvantaged students pay for uniforms
V. Conclusion and recommendations

···

TIP: Check and double-check every paragraph of your essay to make sure
that each paragraph either supports or expands on your thesis statement.

···

HOW TO ORGANIZE YOUR ESSAY

Both informal and formal outlines are tools for planning the order in which you
will assemble the information and ideas you plan to include in your essay.
However, the outlining process is really simply the written device you use to put
in order the information and ideas you have decided to include.

There are many useful strategies, or systems of presentations that you can
choose among for presenting your material. Keep in mind that you may use
these various strategies for individual paragraphs in your essay, or you may
extend them to use throughout the essay.

Here are some common organizational systems or patterns to remember:

Sequential or Chronological Order. Use this system when you want to
describe events in the order in which they occurred or when you want to
describe a process, such as a recipe or a trip, which can best be explained in
sequential order.

Cause-and-Effect Order. This is an ideal organizational strategy to use
when you want to describe an event or a situation and how it came to be. For
example, if you are asked to write about the career of your favorite sports figure, you might want to begin by writing about the athlete's childhood, and then
go on to trace the influence of childhood training on his or her eventual path to
stardom.

···

TIP: When choosing to use the cause-and-effect strategy, remember that
most events have more than one cause, so you'll need to be careful not
to simplify your description of events. Readers are always on the alert
to catch writers who have left out important or relevant information.

···

Spatial Order. Writers often use this strategy to describe a place or an
object. Imagine, for example, that you are asked to write a description of the
block you live on, or the structure of the Eiffel Tower. Spatial order works best
when you take the reader around the object in some logical path (left to right,

top to bottom, north to south) that allows the reader to visualize the place or object you are describing.

General-to-Specific Order. This is a strategy that works in a lot of writing situations. You start your essay with the most general information about your subject and then move on to more specific parts of the topic. This is the strategy used in the formal outline you read earlier about the school uniform controversy. Look back at that outline and you will see that the information presented starts with the very general (national statistics) and moves to the very specific (interviews with proponents and opponents of the idea).

....

TIP: No matter which organizational system you are using, your main goal must be to make it easy for the reader to follow along with you. Your job is to act as a kind of guide, showing your reader the way through your argument. At the end, your reader should be in complete agreement with your thesis statement, because you have taken him or her step by step along the path of your argument.

....

PRACTICE 1: WRITING ROUGH OUTLINES

Go back to the thesis statements you created in Lesson 13. Choose one of your statements and write a rough outline for an essay on that subject using one of the four organizational strategies described in this lesson.

Remember that you have already written introductory sentences (or paragraphs) for your thesis statements, so this first part of your rough outline is already partly written.

additional organizational strategies

Good writing is always a breaking of the soil, clearing away
prejudices, pulling up of sour weeds of crooked thinking,
stripping the turf so as to get at what is fertile beneath.

BLAISE CENDRARS (1887–1961)
SWISS NOVELIST AND POET

This lesson supplies you with additional helpful strategies for organizing your writing. In Lesson 14, you learned about some of the most common ways to organize the material in an essay. In this lesson, you'll explore additional ways to organize your ideas and information.

ORDER OF IMPORTANCE. This system of organization is frequently used, and is quite similar to the general-to-specific system that you read about in the previous lesson. You can use this system when you have a major idea or a shocking statement that you want to begin with, and then go on to develop ideas out of your bigger statement as the essay progresses.

When you think about it, you'll realize that most individual paragraphs are organized this way, with a topic sentence that is most general, or inclusive, followed by supporting sentences that elaborate upon the general statement. You can also use this pattern backwards (you might even say upside down) by starting a paragraph or a section with the least important information and then working up to a strong statement supporting your thesis. If you build your argument in this upside-down way, you are guiding the reader, point by point, and slowly but surely convincing him or her to agree with your argument. (Think of how you construct an argument when you are asking your parents for something you think they might not want to give you. Isn't this the pattern you use in trying to convince them to come around to your way of thinking?)

Classification or Analysis. The lesson you are currently reading, and the one that precedes it, are good examples of organization by classification. What you are reading here is a list of types of organizational strategies; these lessons have created a classification system for you, the reader. Notice how much easier it is to learn about several types of writing strategies if they are presented to you in a list, with headings to separate them. Consider incorporating a list and headings into essays that you write in the future. They are useful devices—efficient signposts to help the reader stay interested.

Often you can use the classification strategy in essays where you are writing about several parallel things or ideas. For example, what if you were asked to write an essay about the various classes that you take each day? Couldn't you classify them by class period? Or subject matter? Or size of the classroom? Or even by how much you like (or dislike) the teacher? All of these ways to organize your ideas are actually using a classification system to present ideas.

The analysis part of the classification system appears in the details of your presentation of ideas. For example, if you have created a classification system for the various classrooms you visit every day, your explanation of the variations among those classrooms would constitute your analysis of the separate elements in your system. If you are describing your teachers, your descriptions of why you like certain teachers are really your analysis of the qualities that you think make a good teacher.

Problem and Solution. This organizational principle is fairly obvious. You present the problem and then you offer a solution. Your job as writer is to state the problem clearly enough, and interestingly enough, that the reader will want to keep reading, and will agree with the solution you offer. For example, imagine that you have been asked to write an essay about global warming. Where would you start and how would you organize in such a way as to retain the reader's interest? One obvious organizational plan would be to begin by describing the problem and then offering a list of ways in which the reader could participate in solutions to the problem, for example, conserve energy, do more recycling, drive a hybrid vehicle, save more trees. You could then end with a strong statement convincing readers to get involved personally and do something about global warming.

Compare and Contrast. You've probably heard of this strategy; it's a favorite with lots of teachers because it's a good way for students to tackle the problems of organization in a fairly simple way. First, of course, you must be comparing ideas, objects, or events that share significant points of comparison. It wouldn't make sense to compare and contrast completely unlike things, such as jumping rope and driving a car. But you could easily compare driving a car and piloting a plane.

Let's assume you are going to compare driving and piloting. There are a couple of ways you could organize the comparison.

Organizing Consecutively. In this instance, you would first discuss all the aspects of driving a car, such as training techniques, observing safety rules, observing road signs, managing passengers, and so on. Then you would separately discuss all the aspects of flying a plane. And then you would perhaps write a conclusion in which you summarize the similarities and differences between the two tasks. This organizational structure would probably work, but it isn't exactly fascinating. You're asking the reader to stay with you for a long time before you get to the interesting part in which you actually compare the two tasks.

Organizing Point by Point. A better way to organize the essay about driving and flying would be to compare and contrast individual aspects of the two things. For example, you might compare and contrast the age requirements of both tasks, then the training requirements, and then the safety issues involved in each. And you could end with a comparison of the thrill and danger involved in both. Do you see how using this point-by-point strategy is likely to create a more interesting essay? One that holds the reader's interest and offers you a path to an impressive ending?

PRACTICE 1: CHOOSING ORGANIZATIONAL STRATEGIES

The following chart offers several essay topics that you might be asked to write on. For each subject, suggest the organizational strategy that you think might work best.

Consider carefully. The obvious solution might not be the best solution. And don't forget to look back at Lesson 14 to review the strategies described there.

Essay Topic	Organizational Strategy to Use
the contents of my school locker	
cats and dogs	
the place of the Internet in my life	
my favorite television show	

---

the pyramids of Egypt

---

using digital cameras

PRACTICE 2: REVISING YOUR ORGANIZATIONAL STRATEGY CHOICES

For this exercise, pretend that your teacher has looked at the choices you made in Practice 1, and she says that your choices don't reveal sufficient imagination or originality. Revisit the chart and suggest different organizational strategies for each of the essay topics.

Completing this exercise should remind you that there is always another way to organize the essay you're planning.

Essay Topic	New Organizational Strategy to Use
the contents of my school locker	
cats and dogs	
the place of the Internet in my life	
my favorite television show	
the pyramids of Egypt	
using digital cameras	

common essay types

I write rhymes with addition and algebra, mental geometry.

ICE-T (1958–   )

RAPPER, ACTOR, AND WRITER

In this lesson, you'll learn about the three most common essay types: expository, persuasive, and narrative.

IN LESSON 13, we discussed the three essential parts of every essay (introduction, body, and conclusion). In Lessons 14 and 15, we explored various strategies for organizing your essay. Now you will learn about the most commonly used essay formats. This lesson gives you practice in planning how to achieve your communication goals by choosing the best essay format for what you actually want to say.

In general, there are three types of essays that are most commonly assigned in middle school, high school, and college. (We will not take up the writing of research papers here because those projects involve a different set of more complicated rules and procedures.) In almost every case, essays you are assigned, or even those you choose to write on your own, will fall into one of the three following formats.

EXPOSITORY ESSAYS

Expository essays are probably the most frequently assigned format for students. This essay format requires the writer to explain something to the audience. Specific expository writing assignments might include the following:

- describe a process (how to bake a cake)
- compare and contrast two ideas or things (compare cats and dogs as pets)
- explain a cause-and-effect relationship (pollution results in global warming)
- review something (favorite movie or book)
- define (how corn grows; how caterpillars become butterflies)
- discuss (future developments in technology)

As you can see by these examples of expository assignments, the writer's task is to provide exposition, or inform the reader about the assigned subject, which may include providing examples, facts, relevant anecdotes, as well as personal knowledge the writer may have about the subject. Once the writer has clarified the subject to be explained, he or she is free to choose among the many organizational strategies we explored in previous lessons.

PERSUASIVE ESSAYS

Persuasive essays are the second-most common essay format that you are likely to be assigned. In this format, your task is to convince the reader of your point of view on some subject; alternatively, you may be required to convince the reader to take some particular action, such as vote for your candidacy for class president. Here are sample essay topics that require the persuasive essay format:

- Skateboarding should be prohibited on city streets.
- Violence on television is resulting in violence on our streets.
- The voting age for national elections should be raised to 21.
- Presidential terms should be extended to six years in order to give sitting presidents more time to enact their policies.

As with all other essay formats, it is essential in a persuasive essay that you define your topic narrowly; construct your thesis statement precisely; and offer statistics and facts as well as opinions to support your argument. Additionally, you will make a more persuasive argument for your position if you are knowledgeable about and acknowledge the other side of the argument in your essay.

NARRATIVE ESSAYS

Narrative essays tell a story, or report an event, or describe an experience. Usually, but not always, narratives are told from the writer's point of view. Like other essay formats, narrative essays must include a point, a thesis statement that engages the reader as well as sufficient vivid details to make the story come alive.

Not all narratives are written in the writer's voice. You could easily write a narrative in the voice of a character you have invented, or indeed, in the voice of a historical person. (For example, you could write an imaginary letter from George Washington to his parents.) Here are sample essay topics for which you might use the narrative essay format:

- If I could have a super power, it would be _____.
- Are there still heroes to admire?
- the best advice I ever got
- surviving a tornado
- How would you reduce crime in urban areas?

Narrative essays are an ideal place to apply the 5 W questions: *who, what, where, when,* and *why.* Because narrative essays are often personal stories, or at least ideas presented using the first person (*I believe that . . .*), you must be sure that you are writing from a thesis statement. Your thesis statement might not be actually spelled out in your first paragraph, but it must be the guiding principle that makes this story of interest or value to the reader.

Often narrative writers conclude their essays with a summary statement, such as *And so I learned from this* _____ *experience, never to trust* _____. Another conclusion of this type might be *Be careful, then, when you wish for a super power. My experience having such a power proved* _____.

APPLYING COMMON ESSAY FORMATS TO OTHER WRITING PROJECTS

While this lesson has concentrated on essays you might be assigned as class-work, these formats are perfectly adaptable to other forms of writing projects. Here are other ways in which you might use these formats.

- **Journal writing.** Nothing improves your writing as much as prac-tice. Experiment by writing in the expository form for ten minutes every night for a week. Choose a topic every night and try to write in the third person instead of writing in the first person, which is the one most often used by journal keepers. If no subjects come to mind immediately, use one of the sample expository formats pro-vided in this lesson.
- **Poetry.** Poems don't have to rhyme, and they don't have to be about love, or pain, or any personal feelings for that matter. If you've never written a poem, try to write one. If you start by choosing a surprise format, such as the persuasive format, you may have fun writing in a new way.
- **Text messaging or instant messaging.** Instead of writing texts of messages in your usual personal narrative format, try writing your next text or IM in an expository format. Write to your friend and explain something—anything—and see how workable that format can be.
- **Songs.** Even if you're not a musician, you may be a lyricist (a person who writes the words of songs). Try applying what you've learned about creating a strong thesis statement supported by relevant details to the practice of writing lyrics for a song. You may have fun.

PRACTICE 1: WRITING STRONG THESIS STATEMENTS

In this exercise, you will practice writing strong thesis statements for sample essay topics. In addition to proposing a thesis statement, include the essay for-mat that you think would work well for your thesis.

Choose your favorite three topics from the sample topics provided in this lesson, and write concise, clear, meaningful thesis statements for them.

A chart and sample are provided to help you.

Essay Topic	Thesis Statement	Essay Format to Use
If I could have a super power. . . .	Flying, frankly, is a highly overrated super power.	expository

PRACTICE 2: WRITING ABOUT THE FIRST DAY OF SCHOOL

In this exercise, write a first sentence in each of the three essay formats discussed in this lesson about the same subject. The purpose is for you to experiment treating the same event in several different ways.

Think about the first day of school—your own first day or someone else's. It can be preschool, kindergarten, or any other grade. Now write interesting, engaging first sentences for each type of essay format.

Essay Format	First Sentence (or Paragraph)
expository essay	
persuasive essay	
narrative essay	

writing to prompts

If I can say something honest about my feelings and thoughts and problems as a minority of one, then won't it be meaningful to all the other individual minorities of one?

DORY PREVIN (1929–)
AMERICAN SINGER AND SONGWRITER

This lesson will help you learn how to respond to the various writing prompts your teachers are likely to assign. In addition, you'll learn how to adapt to other writing situations.

BY NOW YOU should be feeling fairly comfortable with the various types of essay formats and the organizational steps you need to take at the beginning of any writing process. In this lesson, you'll learn strategies and tips for responding to assigned prompts.

For the great majority of writing projects you do as a student, you will be writing in response to assigned prompts. A **prompt** is a word that describes the question you are being asked to answer or the writing assignment you are given. Some teachers use the word *prompt* and other teachers use the word *assignment*. Both mean the same thing. As you are aware, writing prompts can require you to write in numerous and varied situations:

- in-class writing sessions, either formal essays or informal journaling and freewriting
- homework assignments
- standardized essay tests, including grade-level exit exams

In addition to these formally assigned prompts, think of all the situations in which you find yourself writing in other formats that require you to conform to explicit or implicit expectations. Such writing situations include

- writing letters, including thank-you notes
- answering questionnaires
- filling out forms
- constructing your Facebook page
- texting your friends

When you stop to think about it, you'll realize that there are almost no situations, except perhaps freewriting, in which you are writing without some expectations of what your writing will look like, either in form or in content.

The basic principles of what constitutes good writing remain constant of course, but the specifics of any given assignment can have a great impact on what and how you choose to write. In that sense, every writing project is unique and requires expert tailoring if it is to succeed in its goal of communicating effectively. Here are guidelines to follow in your writing process, no matter what the specific assignment is.

TAKE TIME TO PLAN

What may surprise you is that the most important portion of the time you spend on any writing assignment is not the time you spend writing. Rather, it is the time spent preparing to write. Taking the time to prepare properly, which includes taking time to consider carefully what the prompt expects of you, is the most valuable time you will spend on any writing task. Resist the temptation to start writing immediately, just to get your project over with. In the end, your essay will be better, and will take less time to write, if you've devoted a certain amount of your writing time to thinking and planning.

Timed essays, such as the ones you are asked to write during a specified amount of time during class, are usually the ones that strike terror in the hearts of most writers. There is a natural tendency to feel panicky, and to want to start scribbling right away. Resist that urge! Instead, stop and think and plan. Your best bet is to assign a certain percentage of the time you are allotted to be used solely for planning. This planning time will make the remainder of your writing time less stressful and more productive.

Indeed, you cannot go wrong as a writer if you think of every writing assignment as a timed assignment. Instead of fiddling around, complaining about the assignment, postponing getting down to work, and then interrupting your writing time with texting, phone calls, snacks, errands, anything to avoid getting down to the work at hand, try this: Establish a time (half an hour, one hour, two hours) in which you will get your essay written, set the timer, and begin. You'll have a time goal as well as a writing goal to reach, and you'll be thrilled when the time is up and the work is done.

- Budget your time within the writing period you have decided on. Remember to leave enough time to edit and revise.

Using your time carefully will help you stay on track. You'll have a schedule to keep as well as a writing goal to reach, and you'll be thrilled when the time is up and the work is done.

ANALYZE THE PROMPT

The first part of your planning time should be used to analyze carefully the intent of the prompt. In general terms, writing prompts are assignments; they suggest topics for your writing. Sometimes they are general and open-ended (Write about your favorite book), and other times, they are complex and present a topic that demands that you respond more or less in a specified way (Write a defense or a refutation of the following statement: *The moon is made of cheese.*)

Thus, your first task is to decide exactly what is being asked of you. Ask yourself these questions:

- Is the prompt structured in such a way that you will need to organize your essay in a certain format?
- Is the prompt designed to have you take a position on a controversial issue and defend your position?
- Is the prompt open-ended and general?
- Is the prompt asking you to write in a certain format, for example, a persuasive or an objective expository essay containing lots of factual evidence?
- Does the prompt allow you to reject the obvious response and find a way to go around the prompt and write your essay in a totally different way, perhaps by attacking the question?

PRACTICE 1: CHOOSING A RESPONSE TO A PROMPT

Describe briefly how you would respond to the prompts listed here. In 15–20 words or fewer, explain the kind of essay the prompt is suggesting you write.

Include a description of the kind of details or organizing strategies you would use. Remember, there are no right or wrong answers, but there are both intelligent and careless answers. So, think before you write.

Writing Prompt: Should smoking be banned in all restaurants?

Response I'd Make:

Writing Prompt: What is your pet peeve?

Response I'd Make:

Writing Prompt: Why is *To Kill a Mockingbird* a powerful book?

Response I'd Make:

Writing Prompt: How and why do bees make honey?

Response I'd Make:

WRITE AN OUTLINE: FORMAL OR INFORMAL?

When told to write an outline, students frequently respond in one of two ways:

- I don't have time to write an outline.
- I don't know what I'm going to write until I start writing.

Both of these are faulty responses that will not contribute to your ease or efficiency as a writer. Take time to do a bit of outlining, even if all you write in advance is the kind of rough informal outline you learned about in Lesson 14. (If you can't remember what an informal outline looks like, go back right now and reread Lesson 14; that will be time well spent.)

If you are really, truly pressed for time, at least take a few moments to write down the following:

- Your thesis statement. It is essential that you have this in writing in front of you at all times during the writing process. Refer back to it throughout your essay to make sure that every sentence you write supports your thesis.
- The two or three main ideas you plan to cover in your essay. You should have these well in mind before you begin writing.
- The conclusion you want to draw. Your conclusion needs to be more than a simple restatement of your thesis statement. The conclusion should be an idea or statement developed out of and expanding upon your thesis statement.

RECHECK YOUR FINISHED ESSAY AGAINST THE PROMPT

Once you have written your essay, go back and take a good hard look at the writing prompt. Make sure that you have responded to it precisely.

- Have you covered all the points the prompt asks you to cover?
- If the prompt asks to you agree or disagree, does your essay clearly take a stand?
- If the prompt asks you to justify your position with evidence from two or more sources, have you done so?
- Have you included a clear thesis statement and a coherent, convincing conclusion?

If you have answered *no* to any of these questions, you must go back and correct your essay. If you've analyzed the prompt thoroughly during your planning time, and used your planning time well, your answer to all of these questions should be *yes*.

WHAT YOUR READERS WILL LOOK FOR

Your reader, no matter who that may be, will be judging your writing with high standards in mind. Even if it's your grandmother reading your thank-you letter, or your Facebook friends reading your description of last night's party, your reader(s) want you to deliver something interesting, informative, and fun to read.

As you write, keep in mind that your reader is asking certain questions and looking for certain qualities in your writing:

- Did you convince the reader to agree with your position?
- Did your argument develop logically?
- Did you make spelling and/or grammatical errors?
- Is your writing lively, vivid, and interesting? Or is it obvious, dull, and clichéd?
- Most important of all, did you write well enough so that the reader is engaged and wants to keep reading to the end of your essay?

S E C T I O N 5

writing your first draft

YOU'RE READY TO write now, but to provide an extra helping of confidence, the first lesson in this chapter includes a quick review of the five most common grammatical errors. Armed with this useful advance preparation, you'll be able to plunge into the actual business of putting pen to paper, or fingers to the keyboard. Just as getting ready to write often feels like the hardest part, writing that first paragraph can often feel like a mountain you can't climb. Relax. You can make it. Just proceed slowly and carefully through the lessons that follow. They'll teach you how to write a strong introduction, support your thesis statement, and build your essay toward a dramatic conclusion. By the end of the section, you'll see how to reach your writing goal, ledge by ledge, step by step, word by word.

review of the five most common grammatical errors

> *My attitude toward punctuation is that it ought to be as conventional as possible. . . . You ought to be able to show that you can do it a good deal better than anyone else with the regular tools before you have a license to bring in your own improvements.*
> ERNEST HEMINGWAY (1899–1961)
> AMERICAN NOVELIST

You can never be too careful about grammar. This lesson provides a review of the errors you are most likely to make and advice on how to avoid them.

BEFORE YOU TACKLE the subsequent lessons in Section 5, concentrate very carefully for 15 minutes on this lesson's review of the five most common grammatical errors. With these reminders fresh in your mind, learning new strategies for the drafting process will be easier and lots more fun.

TIP: If this quick review doesn't feel sufficient, go back to Lesson 6 for more detailed explanations of these common errors.

COMMON ERROR 1: INCORRECT NOUN-VERB AGREEMENT

The Correct Rule: In every sentence you write, the noun and the verb must agree in number. This means that a singular noun must be paired with a singular verb, and a plural noun requires a plural verb. (For a review of exceptions to this rule, return to Lesson 6.)

Incorrect Noun-Verb Agreement: The dog and the cat, sworn enemies, is the funniest dinnertime show at our house.

Correct Noun-Verb Agreement: The dog and the cat, sworn enemies, are the funniest dinnertime show at our house.

COMMON ERROR 2: INCORRECT VERB ENDINGS

Correct Verb Endings: Every verb has four basic parts that indicate the time in which the action of the verb is happening. These four parts form the building blocks with which writers and speakers can describe actions that

1. are occurring in the present
2. are occurring in an ongoing time
3. occurred in the past
4. have or had occurred at some time in the past

All options are covered by these four parts.

Here's a chart to remind you how the verb forms work:

Sample Verb	Present	Present Participle	Past	Past Participle
regular verb	talk	(is) talking	talked	(has) talked
irregular verb	speak	(is) speaking	spoke	(has) spoken

Note that there are many irregular verbs, whose parts you must memorize. Most of the memorizing gets done without thinking about it. In the course of reading and listening to others speak, most people absorb the irregular verbs quite naturally and don't have to stop to think about which form of the verb to use. For example, do you have to interrupt yourself to think when you're talking about a lesson you had in the past? Probably not. You would simply say, without hesitating, "The teacher taught us the lesson." Saying "The teacher teached us the lesson" would not come naturally to you.

Here are some common irregular verbs that you should be careful to use correctly both in your speech and in your writing.

Present	Present Participle	Past	Past Participle
bring	bringing	brought	(has) brought
drink	drinking	drank	(has) drunk
shine	shining	shone	(has) shone
shrink	shrinking	shrank	(has) shrunk

Confusing Verb Pairs

There are some verbs that sound similar but actually mean different things. These verbs probably cause the most confusion in both written and spoken English. Here are two of the most troublesome:

Lie and Lay

Lie takes no object. It describes the act of resting in one position.

Lay takes an object. It describes the act of putting something somewhere.

Lie down and dream of the day when you will be able to lay your grammar book aside and write easily without it.

Present	Present Participle	Past Tense	Past Participle
lie The cat lies down.	lying The cat is lying down.	lay Yesterday, the cat lay down.	lain In the past, the cat has lain down.
lay The boy lays the book aside.	laying The boy is laying the book aside.	laid The boy laid the book aside.	laid The boy has laid the book aside.

Sit and Set

Sit does not take an object. It describes the act of being seated somewhere.

Set takes an object. It describes the act of placing something somewhere.

Set aside your prejudices against classical music, and sit down to listen to this Mozart CD; you may like it.

Present	Present Participle	Past Tense	Past Participle
sit	sitting	sat	sat
The cat sits on the floor.	The cat is sitting on the floor.	Yesterday, the cat sat on the table.	In the past, the cat has sat there for hours.
set	setting	set	set
The boy set the book aside.	The boy is setting the book aside.	The boy set the book aside.	The boy has set the book aside.

COMMON ERROR 3: INCORRECT PRONOUN–ANTECEDENT AGREEMENT

The three most common errors in the use of pronouns are the following:

1. You fail to have the pronoun agree in number with its antecedent (the noun it is replacing or referring to).

    One <u>cat</u> sat staring at <u>her</u> prey. (correct agreement of singular subject and singular pronoun)

    Two <u>cats</u> sat staring at <u>their</u> prey. (correct agreement of plural subject and plural pronoun)

2. You fail to have the pronoun agree in person with its antecedent.

    Each <u>cat</u> had <u>its</u> eyes glued on <u>its</u> prey. (correct agreement)

    Each <u>cat</u> had <u>their</u> eyes glued on <u>their</u> prey. (incorrect agreement)

3. You fail to have the pronoun agree in grammatical function with its antecedent.

    <u>We</u> writers have to be very careful about <u>our</u> pronoun usage. (correct subjective usage)

    <u>Her</u> and <u>me</u> sometimes forget to check our pronouns. (incorrect agreement; objective pronouns being used here as subjects)

COMMON ERROR 4: COMMA SPLICES

Comma splices are simply misplaced commas that usually result from a writer's uncertainty, ignorance about commas rules, or just plain negligence. When you write two independent clauses in one sentence, you need more than a comma to separate them. No error is more common than the comma splice; learning to avoid them and/or correct them is the single most significant improvement you can make in your writing.

....

TIP: When in doubt about a comma, leave it out. You have a better chance of conveying meaning without a comma than you do with sticking one in arbitrarily and thereby splicing the sentence.

....

COMMON ERROR 5: TEN COMMON SPELLING MISTAKES AND WORD CONFUSIONS

Because these words are so commonly misused or misspelled, the list provided in Lesson 6 is repeated here in full. You will be judged harshly by your teachers and your readers if you fail to use these words correctly.

1. Accept: verb, to take something
   Except: preposition, but, or other than

   The teacher accepted most of Tim's excuse, except the part about how the dog ate his homework.

2. Advice: noun, describes help you give someone
   Advise: verb, describes the act of giving someone verbal help

   The teacher advised the students to take her good advice and study hard for the examination.

3. Affect: verb, to modify or make a difference
   Effect: noun, a result

   The effect of bad study habits is often seen in a student's school failures, which may affect future opportunities.

4. Bad: adjective, used with linking verbs as well as to modify nouns
   Badly: adverb, in an inferior way

   The teacher feels bad when her students perform badly on their tests.

5. Can: verb, being able to do something
   May: verb, having been given permission to do something

   The students can study harder, but the chances that they will do so often seem slim.

   If the students do well early in the week, the teacher may give them permission to goof off one hour on Friday.

6. Farther: adverb, describes distance
   Further: adjective, describes quantity

   Runners who want to run farther than a mini-marathon need to invest time in further practice.

7. Lend: verb, to provide temporary use of
   Loan: noun, what you give someone temporary use of

   Your best friend may lend you her copy of the textbook, but the loan is temporary until you find your own copy.

8. Like: preposition, introduces the idea of similarity
   As: adverb, suggests similarity, or in the same manner

   A clap of thunder is like an alarm clock; it startles and surprises you.

   Do as I say, not as I do. (correct usage)

   Do like I say. (incorrect usage)

....

TIP: Try to limit your use of the word *like*. It is probably the most overused word in many vocabularies. While it may be acceptable in conversation to sprinkle your comments with pauses and the word *like*, the word should not be used in formal writing as an indication of a pause or an interruption of thought. It is definitely not a word to introduce phrases, or to use when you can't think of what you're going to say next.

....

9. Media: noun (plural of medium), one or more means of communication or expression
   Medium: noun (singular), the use of a system of communication

   The singer's medium is hip hop, and the media have turned him into a television star.

10. Principal: as a noun, describes a manager or executive who manages a school or business department; as an adjective, describes a degree of importance
    Principle: a noun, describes a rule or policy

    The principal of our school insists that we observe the principle of fair play in all our sports competitions.

    One of the principal reasons to write well is to communicate your ideas effectively.

PRACTICE 1: REVIEW OF COMMON GRAMMATICAL ERRORS

Choose the correct word or correct the error in each of the following sentences to review your knowledge of these tricky grammatical usages.

1. The girl and the boy (*take, takes*) special care to handle the puppies gently.

2. The puppies' eyes were dark brown, and (*shined, shone*) with their tears.

3. The veterinarian (*set, sat*) aside his instruments and petted the puppies.

4. Cats and dogs can be taught to (*sit, set*) quietly together and not fight.

5. My cat Sadie carries (*her, its*) toys around and places them in (*their, there*) secret hiding places.

6. My dog Frank has had a very hard time (*accepting, excepting*) Sadie's rules about dinnertime.

7. All the kids in the neighborhood felt (*bad, badly*) when we lost our pet snake.

8. Having pets is a really good way to teach younger kids in the family, to be responsible and care for others.

9. Sadie and Frank have actually become best friends, and they often (*lie, lay*) down together for afternoon naps.

10. I like swore to my mother that I would take care of feeding a snake if we got a new one.

ANSWERS

Practice 1: Review of Common Grammatical Errors

1. take
2. shone
3. set
4. sit
5. her, their
6. accepting
7. bad
8. delete comma
9. lie
10. delete *like*

at last, your first paragraph

Vigorous writing is concise. A sentence should contain no
unnecessary words, a paragraph no unnecessary sentences,
for the same reason that a drawing should have no
unnecessary lines and a machine no unnecessary parts.
WILLIAM STRUNK, JR. (1869–1946)
AMERICAN EDITOR AND WRITER

Finally, it's time to start writing your essay. This lesson will provide instructions
on how to make sure you are getting off to a good start with your first paragraph.

GOOD FOR YOU for being conscientious enough to get to this point in the book.
By now, you've reviewed English grammar, and you've learned about freewriting, brainstorming, outlining, and developing a strong thesis statement. At last, you're ready for lessons on how to begin the actual writing of your first paragraph, which of course is only the beginning of the first draft of your writing project. So let's begin.

BEGINNING YOUR FIRST DRAFT

Every writing project begins with a first draft. To draft means to write first and subsequent versions of what will become your finished writing project. (As you'll remember, to simplify and minimize confusion in this book we refer almost always to what you are writing as an essay, but it might easily be a report, a review, an in-class test, or even a research paper.) No matter which format you are writing in, drafting followed by revising should be your practice. It is a rare writer who can produce a polished finished piece of writing in the first draft.

The purpose of the first draft, of which the first paragraph is the beginning, is to get your ideas down on paper so that you can go back and revise, expand, and polish them up into a finished essay. Think of the rough draft as a framework or a simplified structure built out of the ideas you developed during your planning and outlining work.

THE ROLE OF THE PARAGRAPH

As you are aware, all writing projects include a series of paragraphs—the building blocks of all written work. (If you listen carefully to yourself and others, you'll realize that you actually speak in paragraphs as well. The shifts from one paragraph to another in spoken language are usually indicated with pauses, or questions, or responses from your listener.) Paragraphs are not just arbitrary breaks in your writing; they are created to perform several very specific functions:

- to provide support for the thesis statement of the essay
- to provide additional ideas that contribute to the thesis statement
- to indicate shifts in subject matter, time, or the speaker (if there is dialogue)
- to provide rest for the reader's eyes, a chance to breathe

TIP: Be sure to vary the length of your paragraphs. A series of very short paragraphs will feel choppy or disconnected; in fact they may indicate that a thesis is not well developed. Extremely long paragraphs make reading through them difficult—they seem to take the reader's breath away. Used carefully, one-sentence paragraphs can make a dramatic impact, but be careful not to overdo this strategy.

THE IMPORTANCE OF FIRST PARAGRAPHS

First paragraphs need to be very engaging, so that you grab the reader's attention and keep it throughout the rest of your essay. The first paragraph is actually the only one that you can be fairly sure will get read; if you don't write it well, you may lose your audience right then and there.

Generally, as you learned in Lesson 13, essays are structured in three parts: introduction, body, and conclusion. The first paragraph of your essay might well be considered the essay's introduction. Most writers choose to include their thesis statement in the first paragraph, but this isn't an absolute necessity. You may want to use the first paragraph to set the scene or introduce the problem that you will discuss in the remainder of your essay. What's much more important than stating the thesis in the first paragraph is making sure that the first paragraph is lively and grabs the reader's attention.

....

TIP: If you're having trouble getting started on a strong first paragraph, skip it and begin your writing with the second and third paragraph. Once you're warmed up and clipping along, you can return to the beginning in your second draft and write your first paragraph.

....

REQUIREMENTS OF A GOOD PARAGRAPH

Every paragraph, whether it's the first or the last, must contain the following features:

1. A topic sentence that presents the main idea of the paragraph. The topic sentence does not necessarily come at the beginning of the paragraph. Just as with the thesis statement of an essay, the topic sentence sometimes appears at the end of a paragraph, as a kind of punctuation mark to the paragraph.
2. A series of additional sentences, all of which contain information that support, develop, or amplify the idea in the topic sentence. These sentences provide unity to the paragraph.
3. A smooth and logical flow. All the sentences in each paragraph should connect to each other easily and logically. The reader should not feel any bumps in the road as the paragraph moves along.

....

TIP: Check every paragraph you write to make sure that it has all three ingredients: a topic sentence, development of the topic, and logical flow throughout.

....

HOW TO WRITE A STRONG FIRST PARAGRAPH

Step 1: Write a good topic sentence.

Your topic sentence needs to hook the reader, and therefore, it needs to be strong and significant. It must not simply hint or take dainty steps around your topic. Look at these two sample topic sentences.

1. King Kong is one of the saddest monsters in movie history.
2. I'm going to write about my favorite movie, which is *King Kong*.

Which paragraph do you want to keep reading? Which topic sentence is a strong introduction to the paragraph that follows? Sentence 2 is not very engaging at all. Why should the reader care what the writer's favorite movie is— unless the writer offers a good reason to be interested. Sentence 1 states a position strongly, and invites the reader to keep reading to find out why the statement is true.

Step 2: Support the topic sentence with additional connected and supporting ideas.

Read the following paragraph and think about how it might be improved.

King Kong is one of the saddest monsters in movie history. He lived on an island called Skull Island. He got sent to New York and was exhibited as a monster for people to stare at. He falls in love with a girl named Ann, and eventually, he is killed on the Empire State Building.

This paragraph lacks coherence and fails to develop the idea in the topic sentence. It jerks along without a smooth flow, and jumps ahead to the end of the movie without having explained or supported the idea of the topic sentence, which is that Kong is a sad monster.

Step 3: Create a smooth and logical flow within your paragraphs. Each sentence should be connected to the one preceding it and the one that follows it.

Look at the following revision of the King Kong paragraph and note how much more informative and logical it is.

King Kong is one of the saddest monsters in movie history. At the beginning of the movie, we learn that he is held captive along with terrifying prehistoric dinosaur-like creatures in a frightening, sinister place called Skull Island in the Indian Ocean. Kong seems to be the only gorilla there, so his life is clearly a lonely one. Things don't get dramatically better when Kong is captured and taken to New York to be exhibited as the *Eighth Wonder of the World*.

Note that the revision of the paragraph improves it by adding the following elements:

- more details of Kong's life that suggest loneliness (he lives alone among terrifying creatures)
- more adjectives and specific details that add vividness and color to the picture the writer is painting (words such as *frightening, sinister, Eighth Wonder of the World*)
- logical time-sequence connections between events (*At the beginning* . . . and *Things don't get better when* . . .

The rewritten paragraph has followed the requirements for writing a strong first paragraph. Even if we've seen the movie before, and know how the story ends, we are interested to learn how the writer proves the thesis statement, which is also the topic sentence of the first paragraph. We can expect that the writer will compare Kong to other monsters in order to prove the thesis that *King Kong is one of the saddest monsters in movie history*.

OTHER TYPES OF PARAGRAPH STRUCTURE

Not all paragraphs begin with a topic sentence that is then developed deductively. Here are some other paragraph types that you may find useful:

Descriptive or Expository Paragraphs. Use this type to describe a person, place, or thing. For example, you might want to describe what Kong looks like, or how he moves. Be sure to include details that describe sounds, color, smells, setting, and so on.

Narrative Paragraphs. Use these when you want to report an event or tell a story. Think about the action of the story, the characters involved, and the setting/scene. Such paragraphs usually have a beginning, middle, and end, but it is more likely that you will need more than one paragraph to complete your narrative.

Informative Paragraphs. Often you need to explain how something works or what happened in certain circumstances. Imagine writing an essay in which you are telling the story of your summer vacation. No doubt you would want to include an informative paragraph (or several) that tell how far you traveled, what transportation you used, and how many people were on the trip.

Persuasive Paragraphs. Use this format when you are trying to convince your readers to agree with you about your topic. This type of paragraph appears most often in essays that make an argument or seek to put forth a specific point of view. Think about the King Kong essay in this lesson. The writer's thesis that Kong is the saddest monster in movie history would be well supported by a persuasive paragraph that compares Kong to other monsters in other movies to show that he is indeed the saddest of all.

....

TIP: Vary the kinds of paragraphs you use in your essay to maintain reader interest and to keep your essay lively.

....

PRACTICE 1: CREATING LIVELY TOPIC SENTENCES

Write a topic sentence for each of the suggested topics in the following chart. For each sentence you've written, suggest the type of paragraph that will form the continuation of the paragraph.

Suggested Topic	Topic Sentence	Paragraph Type
the Grand Canyon		
rap music		
school clubs		

supporting your thesis statement

A scrupulous writer, in every sentence that he writes, will ask himself at least four questions, thus: 1. What am I trying to say? 2. What words will express it? 3. What image or idiom will make it clearer? 4. Is this image fresh enough to have an effect?

GEORGE ORWELL (1903–1950)
BRITISH NOVELIST AND ESSAYIST

No thesis statement can stand alone; every one of them needs support. In this lesson, you will learn how to create six types of building blocks to support your main idea and strengthen your writing.

ONCE YOU'VE WRITTEN your first paragraph, and you're confident it introduces your thesis statement with strength and clarity, you can begin drafting the remainder of your essay. The care you took in drafting the first paragraph should be repeated in all subsequent paragraphs. Their role is to support your thesis statement, engage your reader for the remainder of the essay, and ultimately convince the reader to agree with your conclusion.

As you learned in the previous lesson, good paragraphs are built with logic, smooth flow, and detail. You should assume that your reader is willing to be convinced by your essay, but that you will need to provide support to guarantee that agreement in the end. Your goal as a writer is to provide your reader with sound logic and carefully chosen supporting details that strengthen the foundation of your thesis statement and provide lively and compelling reasons to keep reading.

SIX TYPES OF SUPPORT FOR YOUR THESIS

1. Provide Details and Examples

You will help your reader understand (and agree with) your thesis statement if you provide specific examples that illustrate your thinking. Examples can serve many purposes: you might use them to explain, to describe, to respond to assumed challenges from your reader, or simply to provide elaboration of one of your ideas.

In the paragraph from the King Kong essay that was introduced in step 3 in Lesson 19, a few specific details of Kong's life on Skull Island provided support for the thesis statement that he is "the saddest monster in movie history." Sensory details (such as taste, smell, sound, touch) are often effective supports to make your writing more vivid and convincing. For example, in writing about Kong's terror in captivity, the writer might mention Kong's bellowing. Imagining the sound of Kong's fear would help the reader imagine his sadness. Can you think of other details the writer might add to provide more support in subsequent paragraphs?

2. Provide Facts for Support

People tend to believe in facts, which seem to be objective and unchangeable. Because facts are not subjective, they are more easily agreed upon universally. The use of facts in any argument is likely to strengthen the writer's position. (Always remember that every thesis statement is basically an argument asking the reader to agree to the writer's point of view about some subject.)

Facts come in many forms; they can be statistics, definitions, logical conclusions, or carefully constructed observations. For example, to support the argument that Kong has a place in movie history, the writer might provide some facts about the movie's influence in movie history; how many times the movie has been remade; and how many other movie monsters have been patterned on Kong.

It is essential that you include facts or statistics with a purpose. Too many writers make the mistake of including facts without providing a context for them, or without explaining their relevance to the thesis statement. For example, the Kong writer might include facts about the film's length or the kind of film that was used to shoot it, or the date on which the film opened, but these facts are unlikely to be supportive of the essay's thesis. A good rule to follow: Make it relevant, or leave it out.

3. Provide Reasons to Agree

The strongest arguments are usually those that win readers over with the greatest ease, and usually they do so with sound logic, specific examples, and good common sense. When you're building a thesis statement, you will be wise to consider all the reasons a reader might not agree with you, and make sure that you address or dismiss those potential concerns with your own list of reasons why your thesis is a good one.

For example, let's return to sweet, sad Kong. The writer of the King Kong essay must prove the thesis about Kong's sadness with more convincing reasons than that the writer says so. Here are sample reasons the writer might include why we should accept the sadness thesis:

Weak Reason: "I couldn't stop crying at the end of the movie; it was just totally sad." (Too emotional and subjective; not a factual reason to agree.)

Good Reason: "One has only to mention the name Kong all over the world and moviegoers' eyes will tear up. He has become the very symbol of brutalized innocence." (Difficult fact to prove, but a strong, easily accepted semifactual statement.)

Strong Reason: "The multiple remakes of this movie prove the profound emotional impact of Kong on movie history and on the widespread fans and moviegoers." (Easily substantiated fact.)

4. Include Anecdotes and Descriptions

Depending on the type of essay you are writing, it may well be appropriate to include anecdotes of personal experience that support your thesis. For example, if you are writing about a controversial topic such as "Should school uniforms be required?" a personal story about your experience in a school that required uniforms might be helpful. Personal anecdotes can support a thesis best when they relate directly to the topic and illustrate a particular point about the topic. Beware of generalized anecdotes that only indirectly contribute to the argument you are making.

Descriptions of specific events or situations that pertain to your topic are always helpful. In an essay about school uniforms, for example, descriptions of what various uniforms look like and descriptions of schools that have adopted uniforms would be strong information to include—whether you are writing in support of the idea or in opposition to it. Remember to choose descriptions and facts and evidence carefully. A good writer should be able to support almost any argument.

5. Include Expert Opinions and Quotations from Authorities

Consider all the cops-and-robbers shows you watch on TV. How many of them end in a dramatic courtroom scene with expert testimony from a medical examiner or a scientist? Including expert opinions and quotations from authorities is an excellent way to support a thesis statement.

Here's the proper way that our Kong fan might have used a quotation from a film critic who has written an entire book about Kong, *Tracking King Kong: A Hollywood Icon in World Culture.*

In her fascinating analysis of Kong and his influence, Cynthia Erb suggests that:

> Like James Bond, Scarlett O'Hara, Batman, and the Star Trek characters, King Kong has become a cultural phenomenon—a character repeatedly featured in advertisements, political cartoons, musicals, operas, novels, comic books, film sequels, music videos, and other cultural works.

Your expert opinions and quotations don't always have to come from books, periodicals, the Internet, or other published sources. You can interview experts or other interested parties on your own. Be sure you quote your interviewees correctly, and provide the expert's credentials in order to justify your use of the expert's opinion as support for your thesis statement.

6. Include Quotations, Diagrams, or Other Visuals

One of the best writing rules to follow is this: Show, don't tell. What that means in essay writing is that very effective communication often results when you can prove your point with some kind of visual aid in addition to your use of words. When you are writing about a story or a poem, strengthen your points by quoting directly from the text. Here's an example of the way that can be done:

Robert Frost concludes "Birches," his elegant poem about life and its possibilities, with this lovely wistful line: "One could do worse than be a swinger of birches."

Adding a chart, a drawing, or a map to your essay can often add interest and provide useful illustration of your points. Writing on a computer with Internet access enables writers to include photos and other visual aids in their essays. (Be careful to honor copyright rules about using published material from other sources. Just because something is published on the Internet does not mean that it is free for you to use. This subject will be discussed further in Lesson 30.)

....

TIP: Try to include a variety of supporting features in each essay you write. Don't depend on only one kind of evidence; the more types of support you use, the stronger your essay will be.

....

PRACTICE 1: CREATING SUPPORT FOR YOUR THESIS STATEMENT

Now that you've read one writer's opening paragraph about a favorite movie, and read suggestions for support for that thesis, complete the following exercise. Identify your favorite movie, suggest a thesis statement for an essay about it, and then supply three types of supporting material you might include in the essay, with examples.

My Favorite Movie:

My Proposed Thesis Statement:

Three Examples of Types of Supporting Material I'd Add:

1.

2.

3.

---

the five-paragraph essay

The skill of writing is to create a context
in which other people can think.
EDWIN SCHLOSSBERG (1945–)
INTERACTIVE DESIGNER AND AUTHOR

This lesson introduces you to the most popular essay format used in school assignments and standardized tests.

IN YOUR WORK thus far, you have learned the importance to your writing of planning ahead, developing your ideas, creating a thesis statement, and, in the actual writing, supporting that thesis statement with relevant and convincing detail. Now it's time to learn about how to tackle the process of an actual writing assignment.

Every writing assignment of course is different. You might be writing an article for the school newspaper, an e-mail to a friend far away, an entry for your Facebook page, or, most often, you'll be writing some type of an essay for a school assignment. We'll concentrate here on school assignments, but the principles you'll learn can be applied to any type of writing that you are doing.

In fulfilling school assignments, you must, of course, follow instructions carefully:

- Pay close attention to the assignment, and, if instructions are delivered in writing, make sure you understand them before you take them home.

- If the teacher is giving you oral instructions, be sure you take notes and ask questions about any details of the assignment that you're not certain you understand.
- Find out if there is a length requirement or any other specific requirements that you need to fulfill in your assignment.

SPECIAL REMINDER: PAY CLOSE ATTENTION

Understanding the exact assignment may seem an easy task, but failure to do so is one of the most frequent problems in essay writing. Often students haven't bothered to take notes while the teacher was explaining the assignment, and by the time they get around to writing the essay, they're a little fuzzy on what the exact assignment is. So pay attention—you'll be glad you did once you begin the actual writing work.

Once you've gotten absolutely clear on what the assignment is, you're ready to write. Right? No. It's rarely that simple. Your first task is to decide in what format you're going to write. Luckily, there's a classic, time-tested format that you'll find useful in many (if not quite all) of your writing assignments. If you learn this format well now, you'll find writing much less of a troublesome challenge in all your writing years to come.

THE PARTS OF A FIVE-PARAGRAPH ESSAY

This essay format is well named. It tells you exactly what you are to write: an introduction, three body paragraphs, and a conclusion. To require exactly five paragraphs may seem rather arbitrary, but in fact, the format is based on ancient principles of logical argument. You already practiced these principles in previous lessons when you learned about creating a thesis statement and supporting it with details that will convince your reader to agree with the premise of your argument. And your previous practice at brainstorming, freewriting, and outlining should help you plan your five-paragraph essay more easily.

The five-paragraph essay has been used by English teachers at all educational levels for decades; they rely on it because it is a simple way to illustrate the principles of sound argument. Some teachers (and some students) criticize the format because they find it too formulaic, too artificially designed. Other teachers defend the format as a valuable tool that can be applied to a wide variety of writing assignments.

Despite the varying opinions about its structure and its applicability, the five-paragraph essay is an essential template for you to master. Throughout your educational career, no matter what the writing assignment, consider first whether or not you can use or adapt this format to your writing project.

....

TIP: Be flexible in your use of the five-paragraph essay. In some cases, you might not need as many as five paragraphs to make your argument, so use fewer. Or use more. The general structure (thesis → supporting proof → conclusion) is a versatile one that can be adapted to suit numerous assignments.

....

PLANNING A FIVE-PARAGRAPH ESSAY

To illustrate the construction of a five-paragraph essay, let's assume you have been assigned to write an essay about global warming. Here are the steps you'll need to take in planning and writing your essay using the five-paragraph format.

PART 1: THE INTRODUCTION

The first paragraph of your essay should include your thesis statement, sometimes referred to as the premise of your argument. (As you learned in earlier lessons, you might want to delay the thesis statement and put it in the second paragraph, which is of course permissible. But for right now, let's assume you are sticking precisely to the five-paragraph rule.)

Within the first introductory paragraph, you need to do several things:

- Introduce the general topic.
- State your thesis or your point of view on the topic.
- Grab the attention of the reader.

It is here then that you will need to have done your preplanning and selected your topic carefully. You cannot possibly contemplate writing a five-paragraph essay on the gigantic topic of global warming. We'll assume that you've settled on the following narrowed-down thesis statement:

The future existence of polar bears on the planet is in serious danger as a result of global warming.

Once established, the thesis statement must never be abandoned—not even for a single sentence. Every paragraph and every sentence in the remainder of the essay must relate to this introductory statement.

Our writer has staked out a territory, and a position: Polar bears are in danger. The thesis statement has sounded an alarm, and because polar bears are so rare and so universally loved (or are they?), the reader is probably hooked. He or she will want to keep reading and know how and why this is happening, and perhaps what can be done about it as well.

PART 2: THE MAIN BODY PARAGRAPHS

The three paragraphs that form the body of the essay should each focus on a different aspect of the argument. Our polar bear writer might want to devote individual paragraphs to ideas such as these:

- statistics about recent declines in the polar bear population
- explanation of the reason(s) for the decline, such as the melting of the ice pack that supports the polar bear habitats
- examples and anecdotes from animal study groups in Canada and Alaska
- quotations from environmental groups seeking to find solutions to the problem

As you have learned in previous lessons, each paragraph must include a topic sentence and supporting sentences that expand on this topic sentence, which is a kind of mini-thesis. As you begin to write each new paragraph, ask yourself how it supports your main thesis.

TIP: Be sure to create transitions between your paragraphs. Don't jump from one subject to another without creating a logical bridge between ideas. You can do this with phrases such as:

- on the other hand
- another example of this phenomenon
- even before this situation arose
- more importantly

Try to avoid clunky and clichéd transitional phrases such as *In conclusion* and *To summarize*. Instead, make it clear to your readers that you are about to conclude with words and phrases that are an integral part of your argument. For example, you might create a transition to your conclusion in ways such as these:

The single most convincing proof of the problem is . . .

In light of all the factors influencing the situation, the only solution possible is . . .

PART 3: THE CONCLUSION

The conclusion of an effective, high-quality five-paragraph essay does not simply restate the introduction's thesis statement. Instead, a good conclusion presents something more, with some originality, such as:

- an explanation of the importance or significance of the topic to the reader
- an explanation of the controversial nature of the issue (for example, perhaps some scientists claim the danger to polar bears is exaggerated)
- an acknowledgment and refutation of the opposing argument by way of emphasizing your own point of view

The conclusion is the writer's big chance to sew up the reader's agreement. It is the place to make a big splash with a strong restatement of the thesis. This is the last chance you have to summarize your argument and convince the reader of its value—and of your value as a writer.

TIP: The five-paragraph essay is the format used in many scholarship and college application examinations. And it might be the model your parents are still using when they write memos in their jobs. (Ask them!) So, master this format and you'll find yourself using it again.

Practice 1: Designing a Five-Paragraph Essay

For this exercise, you can skip doing the research that would be necessary if you were actually writing an essay. Instead, design a thesis statement within the general topic of global warming and then write a rough outline of the five-paragraph essay you could write on your chosen thesis. (Review Lesson 14 if you aren't certain how to construct an informal outline.)

Title of Essay:

Introduction (Thesis Statement):

Body Paragraph 1:

Body Paragraph 2:

Body Paragraph 3:

Conclusion:

---

writing a strong introduction

Of all those arts in which the wise excel,
Nature's chief masterpiece is writing well.
JOHN SHEFFIELD, DUKE OF BUCKINGHAMSHIRE (1648–1721)
BRITISH STATESMAN AND POET

Learn to begin your essay with a strong introduction, and you're halfway to victory. This lesson provides advice and tips on how to create powerful introductory paragraphs.

WHETHER YOU'RE WRITING a five-paragraph essay, a research report, an entry on Facebook, a contest entry, or a Valentine message to your secret crush, you want to make a good impression. In previous lessons, you learned how to construct an outline, a paragraph, and even a whole essay. In this lesson, we'll look at ways to give your introductory paragraphs the punch you want them to have.

THE INTRODUCTION

Opinions differ as to which part of an essay constitutes the introduction. For some, it is the first sentence of the first paragraph. And of course if you are writing a whole book, you might include an introduction of as few as five or as many as twenty pages, depending on your subject. What's most important is to write an introduction that is in proportion to the whole of the essay. For an essay of three to five pages, an introduction of anywhere from one to three paragraphs is probably appropriate. To simplify our discussion here, we'll consider the first paragraph of your essay the introduction. That said, it's usually the first sentence of the first paragraph that is all-important in setting the tone of your writing project.

WHAT A GOOD INTRODUCTION SHOULD ACCOMPLISH

Your goals in writing the introduction to your essay are similar to your goals for the whole essay. In general, you want to interest the reader and make a convincing argument for your point of view. Specifically though, the introduction has some particular goals. Here are goals for you to seek in writing an introduction to any piece of writing:

1. Grab the reader's attention.
2. State your thesis clearly and concisely.
3. Provide any necessary background information.
4. Establish an appropriate tone and level of formality of the essay.

SEVEN STRATEGIES FOR WRITING AN EFFECTIVE INTRODUCTION

There is no right way to write an introduction. As long as you have met these four criteria, you are more or less free to be creative and imaginative in constructing your introduction. Do pay special attention to the fourth criterion. You need to match your tone to your subject carefully.

For example, if you are writing about a very serious subject (such as global warming), you probably will want to write in formal language, which may be still be personal, but probably shouldn't be full of jokes and slang. On the other hand, if you are writing about your first day at school, you may adopt a very informal tone that includes a good amount of humor.

Here are seven strategies or techniques you might want to choose from to grab your reader's attention.

1. Begin with a shocking statement. The writer in the previous lesson planning an essay about global warming that focused on polar bears might open the essay with a shock like this:

   In 50 years, there will be no more polar bears on the planet.

2. Ask a startling question.

> Are you willing to watch a polar bear die of starvation?

Note that this question combines two strategies: It provides a challenge to the reader and simultaneously shocks with its implicit suggestion that starving polar bears might exist. This is a stronger opening sentence than one that asks, "Is global warming harming polar bears?" That is a perfectly legitimate opening question, but not a particularly strong one.

3. Quote an authority on your subject.

> "In a shrinking ice environment, the ability of polar bears to find food, to reproduce, and to survive will all be reduced," said Scott Schliebe, Alaskan polar bear project leader for the U.S. Fish and Wildlife Service.

Finding a quotation strong enough to serve as your introductory statement can be difficult, but it may be worth the hunt. If you haven't found a good quotation in print, consider doing some telephone interviewing; you may find someone who will give you the kind of quotation you're looking for.

4. Describe an imaginary scenario.

> Think of what the world would be like if there were no more polar bears, no more ice pack, no more Arctic Circle at all.

Be careful when you construct an imaginary scenario; you have to create a believable, if extreme, situation, or your reader will dismiss you immediately as an illogical thinker about to make a ridiculous argument.

5. Begin with an anecdote, personal or not.

> Research scientists in the Canadian Wildlife Service are reporting dramatic declines in the polar bear population. Eyewitness accounts by field workers describe the bears as growing visibly skinnier because they can't find enough food.

It takes a bit longer to begin with an anecdote, but they can be very vivid. Newspaper and magazine writers frequently use this strategy to set the scene for the article that is to follow.

6. Set the scene with interesting background information.

> Global warming may be a difficult subject for the individual to grasp, but field workers in the Canadian Wildlife Service are finding the global problem reduced to a very local level as they conduct their annual demographic count of polar bears in the western coastal area of Manitoba.

This opening statement introduces the general subject of global warming, but quickly brings it to the local level to make the subject more easily grasped by the casual reader.

7. Adapt a familiar quotation or phrase to your subject matter.

> To be concerned about global warming, or not: That is the question facing every person in the world right now, and it's probably the single most important question we face.

This twist on Hamlet's famous speech about the moral choices he faces is a dramatic use of a famous quotation. By using it, the writer assumes that the reader will recognize the quotation, and associate the seriousness of the problem about to be discussed in the essay with the difficult choices Hamlet faces. Finding the right quotation or phrase to suit your subject matter can be tricky, but the search can be fun.

Consider what sort of essays you might introduce with other famous quotations such as these:

- Beam me up, Scotty.
- It's a beautiful day in the neighborhood.
- Happy families are all alike; every unhappy family is unhappy in its own way.
- It was a dark and stormy night . . .
- It was the best of times, it was the worst of times . . .
- Mr. and Mrs. Dursley, of number four, Privet Drive, were proud to say that they were perfectly normal, thank you very much.

WHAT TO DO IF YOU'RE TOTALLY STUCK

Sometimes you simply can't get started on a writing assignment. You don't have an idea in your head of what to write, and you can't think of an opening sentence. The usual reason for this kind of paralysis is that you've procrastinated too long, left the work until the last minute, and now you're panicked. The polite name for this procrastination is *writer's block*, which makes it sound more like a disease than an excuse.

Whatever the cause or the name, there are ways out of this jam. The simplest thing to do is go back to the beginning and start over. Do some freewriting on the assigned topic; that should get you warmed up and focused on the topic.

If freewriting doesn't seem to be working, try creating a concept map. But instead of drawing it in the usual orderly way, make it a crazy one. Create a map with the nuttiest ideas you can think of; these off-beat ideas might lead your mind back to a more appropriate line of thought on the subject.

Another trick to getting jumpstarted is to attack the question. Do some freewriting, or list all the reasons you can think of why this is a bad assignment. You'll soon run out of bad reasons and find yourself adding good reasons to your list.

Whatever you do, concentrate. Unplug your iPod, turn off the TV and the phone, and apply yourself to the task at hand. You'll be so proud of yourself when you finish your writing assignment.

PRACTICE 1: EVALUATING INTRODUCTORY SENTENCES

In the following chart, you'll find pairs of introductory sentences for assigned essay topics. Choose the sample sentence you consider stronger, and write a brief explanation of which introductory strategy the writer is using and why you think it is the stronger of the pair.

Introductory Sentences	Which Is Stronger?	Strategy Being Used
1. I've lived in this town my whole life and never knew there was an underground tunnel.		
2. I've lived in this town my whole life and never knew its best-kept secret.		
1. Baseball is an extremely boring game.		
2. Baseball is so boring it could put the dead to sleep.		
1. The Internet is turning us all into zombies.		
2. The controversy surrounding the effects of the Internet on its users continues to be a hot topic among research scientists.		
1. My favorite movie is Star Wars, for a very surprising reason.		
2. Star Wars is probably one of the five best movies ever made.		

writing a strong conclusion

Say all you have to say in the fewest possible words,
or your reader will be sure to skip them; and in the plainest
possible words or he will certainly misunderstand them.

JOHN RUSKIN (1819–1900)
BRITISH CRITIC AND ARTIST

Finishing up with a big bang is a surefire way to impress your reader. This lesson provides advice and tips on how to conclude your essay with an effective and powerful ending.

WRITING A STRONG conclusion is as important as writing a strong introduction. In fact, you can turn the rules and strategies for introductions upside down and apply them to writing a conclusion. Just as you want your essays to start off with a bang, you want them to end with an equivalent dramatic power.

Perhaps the most common mistake that writers make is to run out of steam and allow their essays to wind down slowly, like a clock losing battery power. The dribble-off ending is the sure sign of a weak essay, and will disappoint your audience and reveal your lack of skill as a writer. This lesson will suggest ways you can avoid this common writer's error and instead construct powerful conclusions that leave your audience with a good impression and the certain sense that you are a skilled and persuasive writer. And incidentally, a strong conclusion may just act as a counterbalance to an argument that isn't been the strongest one you've ever constructed.

THE CONCLUSION

As is true with introductions, there are different views on what constitutes the conclusion of a writing project. If you're writing a lengthy research paper, your conclusion will be correspondingly long and will probably contain a summary of your findings. On the other hand, if you're writing a short essay for a class assignment, your conclusion will probably be proportionally shorter, and no longer than the last paragraph of your essay. Whatever its relative length, the conclusion you write needs to fulfill certain goals.

WHAT A STRONG CONCLUSION SHOULD ACCOMPLISH

As you have learned in previous lessons, every essay is essentially an argument for a point of view. Whether your writing project is a compare-and-contrast, a narrative, or an expository essay, its overall goal is to convince your readers to agree with you because they believe and enjoy what you've written, or agree, with certainty, that your point of view is a correct one. Think of the essay as a first meeting with a potential new friend: You want to make a good impression and leave your new friend anticipating another meeting with you—or in this case, wanting to read another essay written by you.

FOUR STRATEGIES FOR CONSTRUCTING A STRONG CONCLUSION

1. Restate the thesis statement.

   This is the most common way that writers conclude their essays, and the most easily abused technique. Simply restating the thesis is useful as a reminder to the reader, but it can be a very unimaginative device. Be sure not to restate your thesis in exactly the same words. Figure out a way to provide some amplification or a twist that will keep the reader interested.

2. Shine some new light on the subject.

   A strong conclusion provides the reader with some new understanding of your subject. Your essay should lead the reader along a path that winds through a subject area and arrives at a new conclusion. It might be helpful to think of your conclusion as the pot of gold at the end of the rainbow—the gift that the reader will receive for making the journey with you to your concluding argument.

3. Stay on target.

Many writers, in their panic at the end of the writing project, tend to stray off subject and conclude by opening up a new if related subject for discussion. Avoid this trap. Be sure that your conclusion is an extension of your original thesis, and that you do not conclude by suggesting some other topic.

4. Get the reader involved.

An effective way to conclude many essays is to appeal to the reader's emotions. With the use of specific details, you can encourage the reader to make personal associations with your argument and feel the same emotions that you feel about your subject. Another way to get the reader involved is to challenge the reader to consider your argument directly; alternatively, be daring and challenge the reader to dispute an argument you've made very strongly.

SIX MORE WAYS TO WRITE A STRONG CONCLUSION

The right way to write a conclusion is to find the strongest, most effective strategy for convincing your reader to accept your point of view. Challenge yourself to be creative and imaginative in the way you construct your conclusion. Be sure to leave enough time (and energy) at the end of your project for the creation of a clever ending.

Here are six suggestions for strategies to adopt in creating effective conclusions. Note that they are similar, but not always identical to strategies you learned in the previous lesson for writing strong introductions.

1. Ask a question.

A well-constructed essay can often lead to a dramatic question at the end that challenges the reader in effect to contribute to the essay's argument. Imagine that you are writing an essay about the value of standardized tests. The following question might introduce your concluding paragraph and invite the reader to agree with the answer you will then provide to the question:

> "Can we be sure then, at the very least, that these standardized tests are providing valuable information?"

2. Quote an authority on your subject.

Here's a quotation from an authority on standardized testing that might be used to support a thesis, or perhaps even to provide a contrasting point of view:

> "In the February 2007 issue of *Science* magazine, researchers Nathan R. Kuncel and Sarah A. Hezlett of the University of Minnesota conclude that: 'Standardized admissions tests are valid predictors of many aspects of student success across academic and applied fields.'"

As the previous lesson noted, finding an appropriate and relevant quotation might be difficult, but is often an effective strategy for a conclusion. Be aware that you don't have to find a quotation that agrees with you. Maybe a quotation from the opposition will provide a way for you to contradict a known authority and make a strong case for your side of the argument.

3. Provide a relevant anecdote.

Anecdotes are easier to use in introductions, as scene setters, than as strategies for conclusion. However, if you can save the best for the last, your personal experience (or someone else's) might provide a strong punch at the end of your essay.

> The experience of 150 seventh-graders at Centreville Middle School who took the standardized test in English usage is instructive: While 80% of the students were above average students in their class work, only 56% passed the standardized test. Perhaps most damning of all, 53% of the students got lower grades in subsequent months. School administrators attributed this decline in study habits and class attendance to the dramatically lowered morale among the students.

Obviously, this anecdote would work best for an essay critical of the use of standardized tests. Be cautious in choosing an anecdote. Make sure it is not too specific to provide support for your generalized thesis statement.

4. Offer a solution or a recommendation.

Depending on your subject matter, providing a workable and realistic solution may be a difficult challenge. In the case of the assigned essay on the value of standardized testing, one student worked around the difficulty of solving this problem in the following way:

> "Whether or not standardized tests will continue to be part of national policy is at this time unknowable. Nevertheless, there is little doubt that local schools need to enhance their commitment to building writing skills among their students. Without better preparation, students will be ill prepared to succeed in their future lives, much less in the taking of standardized tests."

Note that this conclusion sidesteps the challenge of offering a solution or alternative to the use of standardized testing by concluding that there is a larger, more important issue at stake. This is clever writing and provides the reader with a loftier subject to contemplate.

5. Challenge the reader to action.

In persuasive essays, the use of a call to action is often an effective way to conclude. You must use this strategy carefully, because demanding a specific action of your reader may sound hollow and unrealistic. *Write your congressperson* is an overworked example of this strategy. One of the students writing about standardized testing offered this conclusion:

> "Complaining about the use of standardized tests doesn't get anybody anywhere. These tests are here to stay. The energy that students (and their teachers) devote to criticizing the testing policies would be better spent figuring out ways to beat the tests and perform brilliantly on them. That'll show those test writers!"

6. Make a prediction.

How confident do you feel that you can solve the world's problems? Probably your answer is, "Not very confident." If so, you'll want to be cautious about using this strategy, but three cheers for you if you can find a way to guide your reader to look to the future. Here's what one student suggested:

> Twenty years from now, we'll all look back on the controversy about the use of standardized tests and laugh. The real problem facing schools by then is going to be what to do with the multiple languages our students will be speaking. With the increasing presence of recent immigrants in our schools, schools are going to find that 40% of their students are not native English speakers. Printing standardized tests in many languages will be the least of our problems!

DOS AND DON'TS IN WRITING A CONCLUSION

1. Do consider carefully the goals you seek for your conclusion, and match those goals with one or more of the six strategies presented in this lesson.
2. If you get stuck, take a walk around the block, or sleep on it, and return to the essay the next day to write the conclusion. A little perspective always helps.
3. Do not begin your conclusion with clichéd and trite phrases such as these:

   in conclusion

   to summarize

   I conclude by

   and so we see that

4. Do not repeat your thesis in exact words. Expand on it imaginatively.

PRACTICE 1: WRITING STRONG CONCLUSIONS FOR STRONG INTRODUCTIONS

For this exercise, select three of the strong introductions you chose from the pairs provided in Lesson 22 (repeated on the following page).

Enter those strong introductions in the following chart, and write brief descriptions of your ideas for a strong conclusion to those introductions. Explain which strategy you have chosen to use.

The introductory sentences are repeated here for your convenience:

Sentence Pair 1

1. I've lived in this town my whole life and never knew there was an underground tunnel.

2. I've lived in this town my whole life and never knew its best-kept secret.

Sentence Pair 2

1. Baseball is an extremely boring game.

2. Baseball is so boring it could put the dead to sleep.

Sentence Pair 3

1. The Internet is turning us all into zombies.

2. The controversy surrounding the effects of the Internet on its users continues to be a hot topic among research scientists.

Sentence Pair 4

1. My favorite movie is *Star Wars*, for a very surprising reason.

2. *Star Wars* is probably one of the five best movies ever made.

Chosen Introductory Sentence	Suggested Conclusion	Strategy Being Used

Chosen Introductory Sentence	Suggested Conclusion	Strategy Being Used

S E C T I O N 6

revising your writing

THE SIGH OF relief at having a first draft done and ready for revision is every writer's dream. Once you've finished your first draft, you're ready for the essential next step—the revisions that will make your rough draft into a polished final draft. The three lessons in this chapter show you how to evaluate what you've written against checklists that define good writing. Once revised, your essay is ready for the final polishing steps.

evaluating your thesis statement

Things aren't magically better, if that's
what you're hoping for. It's not that simple.
RANDAL K. MILHOLLAND (1975–   )
INTERNET COMIC AUTHOR

Once you've written a first draft, it's time to begin the all-important process of evaluation and revision. It is essential at this point to understand exactly what is meant by revision. The word *revision* most often refers to the process of reworking, or even completely rewriting, major portions of your work. This may mean rewriting a paragraph, adding new examples, strengthening your argument, or even modifying your conclusion. (The process of improving individual words or sentences is usually referred to as editing.) This lesson focuses on and provides advice on evaluating your thesis statement. Subsequent chapters will discuss the evaluation and revision of the other parts of your essay.

THIS LESSON AND the lessons that follow it explore the second important stage in the writing process: the evaluation and revision of your work. (The first and most important stage is the planning and outlining of your work.) While every writer wishes a first draft could magically be transformed into a final draft, that's an impossible dream. It never happens. The most skilled of writers revise, again and again. Some writers tell stories of having written five or six drafts of even a short essay before they feel satisfied that the work is done and ready to be read by others.

You may not need six drafts, but you certainly should assume that, at the very least, anything you write will require a minimum of two drafts, and that those two drafts will be followed by a last polish; at that point, you will have created, at last, a final draft. That means three drafts at a minimum. Remember, by its very definition, to draft means to create a preliminary version of your work. Successive versions will be smoother and more polished, but your first drafts will always be rough. And that's as it should be.

To help you understand what you should be doing in all those drafts, we'll look first at two common drafting techniques. Depending on the requirements of your writing project, you may find that different kinds of drafts are appropriate. For example, if you are writing a research paper, you'll need to have done all (or most) of your research before you can begin to put any words down on paper. If you're writing a short story, you may feel ready to dive right in. Think about which of these drafts you're most likely to use.

TWO TYPES OF DRAFTS

1. A First Rough Draft

A first rough draft is a document that approximates the assigned length you are working toward; it includes, more or less fully, all the major points you intend to make. If you have prepared adequately, by writing either a rough informal outline or a more formal outline, you'll write a first rough draft from your prepared outline. Most professional writers work from this kind of standard rough draft.

This type of draft reflects all the work you've done in advance of writing it. Before you begin writing your rough draft, you'll have already decided on and written a fine-tuned thesis statement; you'll have in mind several supporting paragraphs you plan to write to illustrate your thesis statement; and you'll have sketched out, however briefly, the conclusion you plan to draw. Your rough draft will utilize all your preplanning, and it will include all the required essay parts: a thesis, a body, and a conclusion. If writing were magic, you'd be almost finished, or at least you'd be hoping so. In fact, once you've gotten this much written, the work of evaluating the first rough draft can begin.

2. The Discover-as-You-Go Draft

Some professional writers insist they cannot stand to write outlines, and they can't wait to get started, so they plunge right in. Most often, these writers are actually practicing a lengthened version of the prewriting technique that you learned about in Lesson 10. These writers can't wait to write an outline first; instead, they write as quickly as they can, discovering, even as they write, the thesis and the supporting details of the argument that they will eventually rework and revise.

This type of drafting can be rather chaotic, and usually results in extended rewrites and extensive editing in subsequent drafts. Another disadvantage to this plunge-right-in approach is that it frequently leads the writer down dead-end alleys far away from the original destination. Writer Anne Lamott calls this kind of draft a down draft, the draft in which you just get it down. She names the next draft the up draft, the draft in which you fix it up.

....

TIP: You will make your writing work much easier if you use the first drafting technique. Don't be tempted to start right in on good writing. It requires advance planning. If you spend the effort and take the time to do this advance planning, your actual writing time will be shorter and less filled with frustration and false starts.

....

BEGINNING THE EVALUATION PROCESS

Before you apply yourself to the evaluation of your draft, you may want to subject it to a peer review. That's a fancy way of saying that you consult with a trusted friend to get an objective opinion about your work. This is not an obligatory step, but it's a very popular one that you may want to try.

There's hardly a professional writer alive who doesn't have a back-up team of other writers who read early drafts and provide feedback, no matter how rough the drafts are. In many cities, writers rent office space together where they can sit side by side and easily compare early drafts. Next time you go past a coffee shop, take a look around; you're likely to spot writers hunched over a small table together comparing rough drafts.

HOW TO CONDUCT A PEER REVIEW

If you choose to have a peer review, select your reviewer carefully. You're asking a big favor: a serious reading of your work that results in thoughtful input. You need a friend you can trust to take on this assignment seriously. Give your friend a deadline (the next day is usually good) and set a time when the two of you can sit together quietly and go over the essay draft together. The job of the reviewer is not to correct your grammar and spelling. The reviewer's assignment is to get an overview of your essay, its thesis and conclusion, its strengths and its weaknesses, and in so doing help you figure out how to start improving it.

Write out for your reviewer a short list of questions about your essay draft to help guide the review process:

- What is your overall impression of the essay? Thumbs up or thumbs down?
- Did it interest you or bore you? (Be honest.)
- Were there places in which you wished for more explanation?
- Did you get confused anywhere?
- Were you convinced by my thesis and conclusion?

During the peer review session with your friend, take careful notes on the feedback you get. (And remember to say thank you.)

BECOMING YOUR OWN BEST CRITIC

Every writer knows, deep down inside, that it is essential to learn how to be a demanding self-critic. In the end, it's you alone with the page that needs revision, and it's your job to make that page better. After taking a break from your essay (preferably overnight) to give your mind time to clear, you must begin the process of evaluating your own work.

Ask yourself the set of questions offered above for use in the peer review. Be strict. Here are some additional questions to ask yourself:

- When I look back at the original assignment, can I honestly say that I have met its requirements?
- Is my thesis statement clearly stated? When I read that thesis statement aloud, does it make sense and does it make a valid argument?
- Have I provided sufficient support in the way of details, examples, anecdotes, and so on?

If you answered *no* to any of these three questions, you need to begin major revisions.

COMMON REVISIONS NEEDED IN FIRST DRAFTS

In most cases, the initial evaluation of a rough draft discovers one of three common weaknesses:

1. **The thesis statement isn't clearly supported by your draft.** It's common for writers to establish a thesis, write the essay, and, in the writing, stray away from the original thesis and provide supporting detail and examples that don't quite fit. The most common revision needed is to tighten or narrow the thesis statement.

   If you decide you've failed to fulfill the assignment, you probably don't need to rewrite the whole essay. It's more likely that you can fix the problem by some minor revisions to your thesis statement.

2. **Your rough draft includes more than one idea.** A fairly common failure of rough drafts is that the essay includes more than one main idea. Often writers get warmed up, and take on more topics than they originally planned. Usually this problem can be solved by narrowing the focus of the thesis statement or by deleting the irrelevant ideas you've included that don't really match up with the thesis statement.

3. **Your essay completely lacks a thesis.** If you've planned and outlined carefully, the least likely and most serious problem that writers encounter at this stage is that they have failed to include a thesis at all. Be demanding in your critique of this draft. If it doesn't seem to make one clear point, or if there is no argument being proved by the essay as a whole, then you will need to do extensive revisions.

The necessity of evaluating your thesis statement cannot be overemphasized. The thesis statement is the linchpin of your entire essay, and therefore deserves the most thorough examination. In the next lesson, we will explore the evaluation of other parts of the rough draft.

PRACTICE 1: EVALUATING THESIS STATEMENTS

Examine the following thesis statements and evaluate them on a scale of 1 to 5 for their strength and clarity (5 is a very strong thesis; 1 is either very weak or not a real thesis at all). Write a brief explanation of the score you have assigned to each.

Thesis Statement	Score 1–5	Explanation of the Score
Office workers make up 20% of the U.S. workforce.		
Some people say there is too little respect for the law, but I say there is too much respect for it.		
Space flight can easily be hazardous to the health of astronauts.		
The eating habits of students throughout the country are beginning to create serious health hazards.		

evaluating your
supporting paragraphs

Read over your compositions, and wherever you meet with a
passage which you think is particularly fine, strike it out.

SAMUEL JOHNSON (1709–1784)
ENGLISH LEXICOGRAPHER AND ESSAYIST

Even a strong introduction can't stand alone. In this lesson, you'll learn tips for
evaluating the building block support you've provided to your thesis statement.

IN THE PREVIOUS lesson, you learned the importance of examining your
rough draft carefully, especially in terms of the degree to which it fulfills the
assignment and includes a valid and strong thesis statement. This lesson
explains the next steps you need to take in evaluating and editing your first
draft. Specifically, you'll review here the hard questions you need to ask yourself and the standards you need to apply to the supporting arguments you have
supplied to prove your essay's thesis statement.

As you know, every essay is really some version of a problem/solution or
a question/answer or a point of view/defense. All that really means is that 99%
of the writing assignments you will have during your lifetime (including memos
you may write once you're out in the working world, or teacher's reports you
may write if you end up being a teacher) demand that you take a strong position on some subject and then persuade your reader to agree with you. That per-
suasion process is essential to the well-written essay. An examination and
polishing revision of the supporting elements in your essay is the second step
in the process of revising your rough draft.

TYPES OF SUPPORT FOR YOUR THESIS

In previous lessons, you reviewed many of the strategies that writers use to support the arguments of their essay. Now you're at the stage where you have to evaluate your own use of supporting material. To help you begin this process, note that, in general, writers evaluate their own work by asking themselves these questions:

- Have I argued in the most persuasive manner?
- Have I offered sufficient support for my position?
- Have I offered a variety of kinds of support?

There is no right way to support a thesis, and there is no precise number of pieces of evidence that you must supply to strengthen your argument. In most of the school assignments that you are given, it is probably wise to assume that a minimum of three supporting pieces of evidence or three related ideas will be sufficient to establish the strength of your argument. But more evidence is usually better, so if you have additional ideas to include, by all means do.

It is important to offer a variety of kinds of support. Your essay will be extremely boring and ultimately weaker if you offer only one kind of support. For review, here's a checklist of various kinds of support that writers often use.

- specific examples that illustrate the thesis
- verifiable facts that support the thesis
- expert opinions on the subject
- expert analyses on the subject
- personal anecdotes from you or others
- persuasive reasons for the reader to agree with the thesis
- acknowledgment of opposing views
- direct quotations from the text if you are writing a literary analysis or critique

....

TIP: Always include more than one (or two) of these support devices in every essay.

....

IS YOUR SUPPORT RELEVANT?

For truly effective writing, supporting material must be relevant. It is all too easy to stray from your subject and include information, arguments, or anecdotes that are merely distant cousins to your topic. Be extremely careful in evaluating your rough draft for this common error.

As an illustration, look at the rough outline below. (You saw a later version of this student's outline in Lesson 14.) Look carefully at this early draft of the outline and evaluate the supporting ideas it includes.

Title: Should School Uniforms Be a Requirement in Our School?

Introduction (Thesis Statement)
School uniforms should be instituted in our school because they will relieve tensions among students and make all students feel equal.

Body of Essay
Paragraph 1: statement of thesis and description of controversy throughout the country
Paragraph 2: list of reasons why school uniforms are a good idea
Paragraph 3: description of the high costs of school uniforms
Paragraph 4: description of negative reactions among some students
Paragraph 5: quotation and comments from a principal of a school that has rejected the use of uniforms

Conclusion
While there has been some serious criticism within the student body about the use of school uniforms, there is good evidence that uniforms do create a more democratic atmosphere and reduce tensions among students. An experiment for a year to try out the use of uniforms seems to be an ideal solution to the controversy.

Does this outline suggest any supporting material that you suspect may be irrelevant or otherwise inappropriate? Look at these criticisms of the outline:

- Paragraph 3, which offers facts about the cost of uniforms, does not provide good support for the writer's thesis. In revision, she might correct this problem by comparing the high cost of uniforms to the often higher cost of regular clothes. Such an argument might support the use of uniforms.
- Paragraph 5 offers a quotation from a principal who rejected the use of uniforms. While it is often a good strategy to acknowledge the opposing argument, this is a tricky way to proceed. One way of making it work might be to discount, in some way, the quotation from this principal. Another might be to add a quotation, ideally a more convincing one, from a different principal, one who supports the use of uniforms.

....

TIP: Be careful when you do interviews. Your interviewees might not turn out to be the people you thought they'd be!

....

CHECKING YOUR PERSUASIVE STRATEGIES

After you've checked your rough draft once to be sure that all the information you've included is relevant, you must do another evaluation of the quality of the persuasive strategies (or tactics) that you've used.

In Lesson 20, you learned six types of support for your thesis. Review them here to make sure that you have used as many types of support as possible in order to strengthen your thesis:

1. provide details and examples
2. provide facts for support
3. provide reasons to agree
4. include anecdotes and descriptions
5. include expert opinions and quotations from authorities
6. include quotations, diagrams, or other visuals

Another very useful way to evaluate the effectiveness with which you've supported your thesis is to ask yourself a series of tough questions. Imagine you're a serious critic, or a demanding teacher, and apply these standards to your draft:

- Is each of the supporting paragraphs very specific and relevant?
- Does the essay establish authority with a strong voice and an appropriate tone?
- Does the essay acknowledge arguments against your thesis and counter them with good evidence?
- Have you supported your thesis with enough information? (Failure to do this is a very common error made by writers in a rush to finish the assignment.)
- Have you double-checked to make sure that you have included no language or generalizations that might offend your readers?

If you can answer *yes* to all of these questions, you've done a miraculously good job of writing your first draft. If you are forced to answer *no* to any of the questions, you're lucky to have guidance about the draft's weak spots. These questions point you to the areas where you need to strengthen your argument, either by expanding your supporting paragraphs or by adding new ones that enhance the persuasiveness of your argument.

It is extremely rare for even a professional writer to be entirely satisfied with a first rough draft. The checklists and questions provide a roadmap to follow in reworking your essay. The hardest part of revising a draft is attacking these big-picture issues. Once you're satisfied that your draft reflects your best efforts to assert, explain, and defend your thesis statement, you can go on to do the detail work of polishing paragraphs and individual sentences. The paragraph detail work of revising an essay will be the subject of the next lesson.

· ·

TIP: If you feel frustrated and stuck about how to fix the problems, give it a rest, overnight if possible, and then come back to the draft with fresh eyes.

· ·

PRACTICE 1: EVALUATING SUPPORTING PARAGRAPHS

In this exercise, you will evaluate three paragraphs one student wrote in support of the following thesis:

The eating habits of students throughout the country are beginning to create serious health hazards.

After reading each paragraph, comment briefly on its validity as a supporting argument for the thesis statement. If you think a paragraph is a good support for the thesis, explain why. If you decide it is not a valid contribution to the argument, make suggestions for how it might be improved.

Paragraph 1

In their rush to get out the door and get to school on time, kids today are very likely to skip breakfast, and that's the worst possible way to start your day. Even a quick bowl of cereal will make all the difference between a healthy start to the day and a long, sleepy morning.

Your Evaluation of Paragraph 1:

Paragraph 2

There are way too many pressures put on kids today. Even in kindergarten, kids are starting to worry about whether or not they will get into a good college. And having the right friends is just as important as getting good grades or doing well at sports. Parents really need to relax and stop creating so much stress on their kids.

Your Evaluation of Paragraph 2:

Paragraph 3

Research shows that 75% of mothers with children under the age of ten are working mothers. What does this have to do with kids' eating habits? Everything! If both your mom and your dad are working all day and come home exhausted, what are the chances that either one of them will have the energy to cook a healthy dinner for the family? The result? Fast food. Take-out. Pizzas four nights out of five.

Your Evaluation of Paragraph 3:

revising the body of your essay

Detail makes the difference between boring and terrific writing.
It's the difference between a pencil sketch and a lush oil painting.
As a writer, words are your paint. Use all the colors.

RHYS ALEXANDER (1978–)
AMERICAN BLOG WRITER

Think of the body of your essay as the meat-and-potatoes of your work. This lesson provides a review of the steps you need to take to revise the body of your essay and make it as strong and nutritious as possible.

IN THE PREVIOUS two lessons, you learned how to take a careful and objective look at your rough draft to check it for big-picture issues. You saw how to analyze carefully the strength and clarity of your thesis statement, and then how to do a similar examination of the essay's supporting paragraphs. In this lesson, you'll learn how to examine your draft minutely to check for the smaller revisions it may need, the all-important details that distinguish effective writing.

IS YOUR ESSAY WELL ORGANIZED?

This is the first big question you should ask about the body of your essay. Presumably you have stated and developed the thesis statement in the first one or two paragraphs of your essay. The body of your essay, all those paragraphs that follow the introduction, are now in need of close inspection. Ask yourself these questions:

- Does the essay flow logically?
- Is it easy for the reader to follow along and see where your argument is going?
- Have you chosen the right organizational principle for your essay?

If you answered *no* to any of these questions, you need to do some serious revisions on the body of your essay. Begin by analyzing whether or not you've chosen the best organizational principle for the essay.

COMMON ORGANIZATIONAL PRINCIPLES

1. **Chronological organization.** This is the organizational system used frequently in narrative essays. When you are telling a story, the natural way to organize is to begin at the beginning. You might also use this principle if you are writing about a historical event, or even one that happened last week. Describing an event from its beginning to its end is commonly found, for example, in newspaper articles.

2. **Cause and effect.** This simple structure is applicable in a lot of essays that seek to describe why something has happened. For example, you might be writing about the gradual disappearance in your school of foreign language classes, and organizing by cause and effect might be the way to trace the development of this situation. You might also use this organizing principle for an essay about some aspect of global warming.

3. **Analysis or classification.** What if you are assigned an essay about all the survival mechanisms desert animals have? Or what if you were writing about the various breeds of dogs and how they compare in competitions? You might use a classification system to organize an essay that describes many categories of things.

4. **Comparison and contrast.** This organizing principle is similar to analysis or classification. For example, if you are asked to discuss the nutritional value of French fries and vegetables, you are likely to compare and contrast them.

5. **Spatial order or order of importance.** Typical in-class writing assignments might ask you to describe the contents of your locker, or the layout of the classroom. For each of these assignments, it might be best to start describing things at the top (or the left or the right) and move around the objects or place you are describing. In an essay about the system of checks-and-balances in the federal government, you might want to start by describing the presidency, and then work your way down to the two houses of the Congress. If you are writing an analytic essay about a painting, you might devote several paragraphs to a description of what you actually see in the painting, by organizing your description spatially, from left to right or top to bottom.

HOW TO REVISE YOUR ORGANIZATIONAL SYSTEM

You may not have consciously chosen one of these organizational principles when you planned and wrote your first draft, but it is likely that one or more of them is evident in your essay. (Go back to Lesson 15 to review organizational strategies in detail if you're not sure which one you've used.) At the revision stage, you must evaluate the choice you made by deciding if the organization of your paragraphs is effective and if it was the best choice you could have made.

For example, imagine that you are writing about cats and dogs as pets, and you decided to write about them in a point-by-point, classification way. You wrote about how they both make good pets, both have four feet, both live happily in families of humans, and so on. Now you read over your essay and it feels obvious, flat, and boring. Maybe a different organizational strategy would improve it. What if you decided to write a comparison-contrast essay about the behavior of cats and dogs? You could easily inject some lively humor and a strong point of view (your preference for one or the other) into such an essay, and still fulfill the original assignment to write about cats and dogs as pets. Or perhaps you could reorganize and write a comparison of cats and dogs to goldfish? Then you could really have fun.

Deciding how to change your organizational principle can be a difficult task. If you feel stuck and can't figure out what to do, carefully inspect the individual paragraphs. Often by analyzing several of your individual paragraphs, and seeing necessary revisions to them, you'll come up with a better idea of how to reorganize the essay as a whole. And sometimes all you'll really need to do is rearrange the order of your paragraphs in order to smooth out its flow.

....

TIP: The organizational principle is the glue that holds the essay together. Make sure your glue is holding tight at all points and that no paragraph has come unstuck and is dangling out on its own somewhere.

....

REVISING INDIVIDUAL PARAGRAPHS

Think of each paragraph as a mini-essay, with a beginning, a middle, and an end. Take a good hard look at each paragraph to see if it has the following elements and performs the appropriate functions.

- Each paragraph should contain one controlling idea. Usually this idea appears in a topic sentence at the beginning or the end of the paragraph. All the additional sentences in the paragraph should relate to this one main idea. If you find sentences that do not relate to the paragraph's main idea, move them out!
- Each paragraph should develop its controlling idea sufficiently. The topic sentence of your paragraph, even if it comes at the end of your paragraph, requires support. If you find paragraphs of only one or two sentences, you have probably not developed the paragraph's idea in enough detail.
- Each paragraph should be directly related to the thesis of the entire essay. Too often writers stray from their original outline and write paragraphs on subjects that do not support the thesis statement. If you find a paragraph like this, cross it out!
- Each paragraph should contribute to the development of the thesis statement. Effective essays create a progression of thoughts that culminate in a strong conclusion. Think of your essay as a rolling snowball: It should get bigger and stronger the further along it goes. If it doesn't, you haven't organized well.
- Each paragraph follows the previous one with logical transitions. You may need only a word or two to create the transition between paragraphs, or you may need a sentence or two. Whatever you do, do not rely on trite transitions like *in summary,* or *on the other hand,* or *in conclusion.* Skilled writers can do better than that.

RECHECKING YOUR INTRODUCTION AND YOUR CONCLUSION

Once you've analyzed and revised individual paragraphs, it's important to take a close-up look at your introduction and your conclusion to ensure that they are as strong and clear as you can make them. Don't be a pushover critic; make yourself revise until these elements are of the highest quality.

Characteristics of a Good Introduction

- provides context so that the reader understands the thesis and its background
- states the thesis clearly and concisely
- establishes the tone or voice of the essay
- hooks the reader's interest

Characteristics of a Good Conclusion

- reaffirms the thesis—in a new way
- provides new perspective on the essay topic
- offers the reader a sense of completeness
- encourages the reader to feel a strong emotion or to feel moved to do something about the topic

....

TIP: Make sure you've completed all necessary content revisions to your essay before you go on to the next lesson, where you'll get tips on how to add polish and shine to your essays.

....

PRACTICE 1: REVISING A BODY PARAGRAPH

In this exercise, you are to revise a sample body paragraph that was included in a student essay on the following topic:

Cell phones should be banned on school property.

The paragraph appeared as the third paragraph in a five-paragraph essay. After you have revised the paragraph, write a brief explanation of what was wrong with it.

Also it is not safe for there to be no cell phones in the schools. When I was in third grade one of the teachers in the school collapsed and had a heart attack. No one in that class had a cell phone so the students and the teachers should all have cell phones and the teacher ones should be paid for by the city so that the teachers can protect the children in case of emergency.

List the paragraph's faults in a few words here:

Rewrite the paragraph here.

S E C T I O N 7

doing the final edit

A REVISED DRAFT, ready for its final polish, is like a cake ready for frosting. The last steps you follow in editing and proofreading your writing are usually the most fun. You get the pleasure of reviewing your work and the extra joy at making sure that every detail is just as you'd like it. Think of yourself as a chef standing back and admiring your work—except for the tiny adjustments you need to make right at the end. The final edit of your writing is actually as important as the first draft; it is here at the end that you make sure your work is picture perfect, with no careless mistakes left for the reader to see. What next? The last lesson of the book provides numerous ideas for how to get your work published—in magazines, on websites, in the local newspaper. After all the work you've put into write well, you should be ready to take the next step and become a published author.

editing your writing

Now is the time in the writing process to imagine that you are the reader, or the teacher. Get out your red pencil and begin editing your work. Look closely; you're after small errors that make all the difference between sloppy and superb writing.

BY NOW, YOU should feel confident about the process of revision. Previous lessons have provided guidance on revising your thesis statement, reorganizing your paragraphs, and refining your conclusion. Now it is time to pay attention to the finer details of your writing; you will now learn how to **edit**, which is defined as the process of improving individual words and sentences in order to ensure they are conveying your exact meaning. This lesson will provide advice and tips on how to edit your document to make it the best it can be.

WHERE TO DO THE EDITING

Are you writing with pen or pencil or are you composing your essay on the computer? Whichever way you do the original writing, it is best to do your editing on paper. When you're looking at the computer screen, it is often difficult to notice your errors. You'll catch more errors, and be better able to see the problems in your writing if you are doing your editing on paper, which is called *hard copy*.

When you're ready to edit, print out your document, pick up your pencil, and keep the following challenging questions in mind as you begin the editing process:

- How many unnecessary words can I find and cross out?
- How often have I repeated myself, saying the same thing unnecessarily just to fill up space?
- How many clichés have I used? Have I used slang or vulgar language inappropriately?
- Have I been pretentious, using the thesaurus to find fancy words?
- Have I remembered to vary my sentence structure?

If any of these questions strikes a chord of recognition, it is time to do some serious editing on your essay. Here are guidelines for eliminating the most common writing errors.

BAD WRITING HABITS TO AVOID

Wordiness

The most common error that writers (even professionals) make is wordiness. This error usually results when a writer is trying to pad the essay, to make it longer to meet a word-count requirement. Be conscious of this bad habit and try to correct it. Wordiness is a sign of sloppy writing, and while you may be relieved that you've met your word-count requirement, your reader will be bored and critical of your tendency to jabber on and on. Note the difference here:

> The students were in an uproar on account of the fact that the teacher had not been exactly cool and had given them an assignment to write essays over the weekend.
>
> The students were in an uproar because the teacher had made a weekend writing assignment.

Repetitiveness

Repeating the same idea two or three times in different words is another sign of sloppy, unedited writing. If you take the time to present your idea well the first time, repeating it will only clutter up the page and interrupt the flow of your ideas. This error usually results when a writer gets stuck and can't think of what to say next. When you come upon such unnecessary repetitions in your writing, delete them. Your essay will be better for it.

Clichés and/or Slang

Have a nice day, Trust me, and *No problem* are perfect examples of clichés—thoughts that have been so overused that they no longer pack any power. If you like, continue to use clichés in your conversation, but definitely avoid them in your writing, which will be fresher and livelier without them.

Depending on the nature of your assignment, it is probably not a good idea to use extremely informal language or slang, which is technically nonformal English. While you and your friends may use certain words frequently and politely, these words may not be known to all potential readers. Note the trite and clichéd use of slang in the first sentence here:

> Homework over the weekend is totally a bummer.
>
> Writing essays over the weekend is definitely not my favorite Saturday night activity.

Slang can create other problems: It can easily confuse or offend others. For example, you and your friends may understand *Get a life* as a friendly put-down, but what if you use that phrase in a persuasive essay and your reader turns out to be suffering a terminal disease? Misunderstandings are easy, so be conscious of possible side-effects your informal language might cause.

Using a Thesaurus to Find Impressive Words

Resist the temptation to fancy up your writing by using a thesaurus. As Stephen King, one of the country's most successful authors, says, "Any word you have to hunt for in a thesaurus is the wrong word. There are no exceptions to this rule." The big words you find in a thesaurus will stick out like sore thumbs in your writing, and make you look foolish and insecure; they can also get you in trouble if you make a bad choice. (By the way, the phrase *stick out like sore thumbs* is a cliché you should avoid.) Your writing will be much stronger if you use naturally simple, clear words. Your ideas are what count, not the length or rarity of your individual word choices.

DEVELOP GOOD HABITS TO IMPROVE YOUR WRITING

In addition to avoiding or overcoming your bad writing habits, here are a couple of important good habits to develop and use during your editing process.

Use Adjectives and Adverbs to Add Precision

In the rush to get ideas down on paper, writers often fail to express their ideas with sufficient precision. As you edit your essay, look for places where you can rewrite simply by adding a word or two to make your meaning more precise and exact. Note the differences here:

My dog and cat fight a lot.
My dog and cat fight fiercely night and day.

Bad weather ruined the game.
A torrential rain interrupted the season's most important game.

Vary Your Sentence Structure

Too often writers get stuck on a sentence structure treadmill. They adopt a sentence pattern and repeat it over and over again. Usually this pattern is "noun → verb → object." While there is nothing wrong with that structure, it gets boring very quickly. Readers want to feel the tempo change. Your writing will be more fun to read, and will get higher grades from your teachers, if you edit creatively and inject variety into your writing style. Note the difference a variation in sentence structure makes in these two passages:

> Writing is not my favorite subject. The lessons are difficult to learn. Reading about writing helps. The rules are easy enough to understand. Using them is a different story.
>
> To say the least, writing is not my favorite subject. I find that reading about writing helps, but the lessons are difficult to learn. While the rules are easy enough to understand, learning how to use them is quite a different story.

Incorporating introductory phrases and other dependent clauses into your writing provides variety in the rhythm of your sentences. Try reading these two passages again aloud to hear the difference between them. Which of the two passages makes you want to keep reading?

The Six Characteristics of Good Writing

Every time you are editing a writing project, check to see if your writing exhibits all six of the required characteristics of good writing.

1. well-developed ideas and content
2. good organization
3. consistent and appropriate tone and voice
4. powerful and engaging word choice
5. variety in sentence structure
6. correct grammar, spelling, and punctuation

PRACTICE 1: EDITING POORLY WRITTEN SENTENCES

Edit each of these sentences to make them more grammatical, effective, and interesting.

Bad   1. He had got it right away that he was in for it.

Better

Bad   2. If your sure you want to help the earth then recycle more.

Better

Bad   3. Fun video games are great to past the time better than writing lessons.

Better

Bad   4. Humankind is able to make the universe significantly better than recent times by exercising a myriad of efforts that hitherto in most instances have been neglected or abused.

Better

Bad   5. My vacation trip was real fun, except for the addition of my family.

Better

proofreading your writing

*Sometimes I think my writing sounds like I walked
out of the room and left the typewriter running.*
GENE FOWLER (1890–1960)
AMERICAN JOURNALIST AND SCREENWRITER

You're in the home stretch now, and the final step is fun. In this lesson, you'll learn how to be a good proofreader. There are tricks here that will help you produce perfect essays every time.

AT LAST, YOU'VE reached the final step in preparing your writing to be read by others. All your efforts at planning, writing, revising, and editing thus far have been focused on getting your ideas down on paper thoroughly and effectively. The last thing you need to do once all the writing and revising are done is proofread, which means checking your document to make sure that no errors in spelling, grammar, punctuation, or formatting have crept in.

This step may be the last, but it is far from the least. If you don't proofread carefully, you risk presenting your work in the worst possible light—full of avoidable errors that reflect badly on your skills and may result in a lowered grade or a negative response from your teacher. As with all the other steps in the writing process, the best strategy is to proceed slowly and carefully. Hold your imaginary magnifying glass in one hand and your pencil in the other, and look closely and critically at your work.

IS IT OKAY TO USE SPELL-CHECKING AND GRAMMAR-CHECKING COMPUTER PROGRAMS?

The answer to this question is *Yes, use them—but with extreme caution*. Computer spell-checkers and grammar-checkers are wonderful aids for the writer, but they make lots of mistakes, and you must never rely on them totally. These checkers are huge programs full of lists of words and word combinations that might appear in written documents; it's as simple as that. The problem with spell-checkers is that they don't think; they simply look for words spelled correctly without regard to their usage. Note this sentence that passed the spell-checker program in Microsoft Word successfully:

> My teacher promise me that she would gave me a good grade.

Technically, there are no spelling errors in this sentence. However, there are two grammatical errors. Can you find them? The sentence should actually look like this:

> My teacher promised me that she would give me a good grade.

The spell-checker does not know that both verbs in the sentence need to be in the past tense. In fact, this sentence also made it through Microsoft Word's grammar-checker, which caught only one of the verb errors in the sentence.

Here's another sentence that the grammar-checking program let slip by.

> This step may be the last but it far from the least.

Note that the second clause of the sentence is missing a verb, and the sentence requires a comma before the word *but*. The program missed both errors, but your teacher wouldn't. Nor would your teacher miss capitalization errors, a common problem for spell-checking programs that don't contain many proper nouns. For example, if you wrote the words *dunkin' donuts*, the program might suggest that the word *dunkin'* is not spelled correctly, but it wouldn't remind you to capitalize this proper name. And of course it would not know that *Dunkin' Donuts* is an actual proper name that is always spelled that way on purpose by the company's owners.

TIP: Never rely on spell-checkers or grammar-checkers. Use them only for a quick run-through on your computer, and then print your essay and get out your pencil to do the real work of proofreading.

HOW TO BE A GOOD PROOFREADER

Professional writers learn, over time, the mistakes they frequently make, and they take extra care to be on the alert for those errors. You may not have had enough experience writing and proofing your own work to be aware of your error patterns. However, there are four common kinds of errors writers make that you should always check for when proofreading your own or anyone else's writing.

1. Check for Run-ons and Fragments

Run-ons and sentence fragments are the two most common errors made by student writers. Do not overlook them; there is no excuse for these in your writing. Reading your essay aloud, slowly, should help you catch any of these your eye doesn't catch on careful reading.

2. Check for Agreement in Your Sentences

Pairing a singular verb with a plural noun, or a plural noun with a singular verb—these are common student writing errors. Here is a typical error:

Jeremy, like most kids, don't want to do homework on the weekends.

Be careful always to note the actual subject of the sentence and pair it with the proper verb. In this case, *Jeremy* is the subject, so the verb in the sentence should be the singular *doesn't*.

You must also be on the lookout for incorrect pronoun use. Students too often pair a singular pronoun with a plural noun, or a plural pronoun with a singular noun.

Jeremy, like most boys, wants their weekends free.

Here the writer has paired a plural pronoun (*their*) with the singular subject of the sentence. It is the plural word (*boys*) in the clause in between the noun and the verb that has caused the writer to make the error. The verb in this sentence is correct. *Jeremy* is the subject of the sentence; he alone is doing the acting.

3. Check for Misspelling of Confusing Words

Confusing words often get missed by writers who are not proofing slowly and carefully enough. Pay particular attention to word pairs such as *your/you're*, *they're/their/there*, *affect/effect*, and *advise/advice*. Similarly, watch out for frequently confused verbs such as *lie/lay*, *sit/set*, and *lend/loan*. Review Lesson 18 to make sure you've got all these confusing pairs straight in your mind.

4. Check for Punctuation and Capitalization Errors

Incorrect punctuation and capitalization are the easiest mistakes to overlook. As you're proofreading, make sure that

- every sentence begins with a capital letter
- every sentence ends with a period (or the correct end mark)
- there are no comma errors
- the first word of a complete sentence in quotation marks is capitalized
- apostrophes are used correctly with possessive nouns
- no sentence ends with an ellipsis (. . .)

BE SURE TO FORMAT YOUR ESSAY PROPERLY

Look back at your written assignment, or recall your teacher's usual instructions, to make sure that you have formatted your essay properly. You don't want to be penalized or evaluated negatively because of mechanical errors. If you are using a computer, make sure that you have adjusted your margins correctly, and that your paragraphs break correctly. If you are handwriting your essay, make sure you have left time to write out a clean, perfect final copy, with no words left out, and no cross-outs or smudges. An essay that looks neat is bound to make a good first impression.

PROFESSIONAL PROOFREADING TECHNIQUES

1. Do not proofread when you are tired and up against a tight dead-line. You are certain to miss errors. Plan to have at least an hour's rest between your last revision and your final proofreading. Ide-ally, let your essay rest overnight before you proofread and print out the final version.

2. Read your essay aloud—very, very slowly. Reading silently at a normal pace is likely to allow you to miss errors. Often the sound of your voice making a verb error, or a pronoun agreement error, will alert you to a problem.

3. Read only one line at a time. Do this by printing out your essay, and then cover it with another piece of paper from the bottom of the page, leaving visible only one sentence at a time. This technique will focus your eyes more narrowly and enable you to consider sentences word by word.

4. Read backward. Publishers use this technique to proofread the text they plan to put on book jackets. Reading backward, word by word, helps the proofreader to catch spelling errors.

5. Slow down. This is the most important strategy of all. Reading aloud in a normal voice or reading silently at a normal rate may not help you catch all errors.

PRACTICE 1: PROOFREADING PRACTICE

Proofread the following passage. Circle and correct all the errors you find. Then list briefly the kinds of errors this writer has made.

Hint: There are ten errors in this very short passage.

My friend Janet and I decide that we would bake brownis to take to the sleepover that our Gossip Girls Club was planning for Saturday night. We look up a recipe on the Internet, and we checked to see if my mom has all the ingredients we needed. Sure enough, everything was their and ready. Then we went into my bedroom to chose what outfits I should wear, and we got distract figuring out a new hairstyle for me. Suddenly the time was late, the cookies never got made we were in a hurry to get ready to go. I guess cookies were just not meant to be that saturday!

a final review

I'm not a very good writer, but I'm an excellent rewriter.
JAMES A. MICHENER (1907–1997)
AMERICAN NOVELIST AND SHORT STORY WRITER

Congratulations on your commitment to improve your writing. This lesson reminds you of things to remember every time you write in order to be totally confident that you have performed all the appropriate steps and done your very best.

AS YOU HAVE learned throughout this book, writing well requires thoughtful planning, observance of the rules of grammar and spelling, attention to detail, and, most important of all, a commitment to thinking hard and doing it right.

This final lesson provides a list of the book's tips that you should remember every time you sit down to write. Review these tips from earlier lessons to make sure you understand and believe them. If you make these tips your own personal rules for writing, you're certain to write better. And remember, it's only taken you 15 minutes a day to achieve this important life skill.

TIP 1: The Single Best Way to Improve Your Writing

The single most effective way to improve your writing doesn't involve writing at all. The secret: Read! If you read (at least) 15 minutes a day, every day, your writing will definitely and magically improve.

TIP 2: Slow Down

The single most useful practice you can develop as a writer is to slow down. Proofread and edit your writing very carefully, and you're certain to catch a lot of errors in advance of submitting your work to other readers.

TIP 3: Learn to Type!

If you don't already know how to touch type, which means typing quickly without looking at the keys, learn how! Being able to type quickly will actually make your writing better—because you won't lose your train of thought while you're searching around the keyboard.

TIP 4: Identify Your Audience before You Begin Writing

The more specifically you have your reader in mind, the more focused and fluent your actual writing will be.

TIP 5: How to Get Jumpstarted

If you're having trouble getting started on a strong first paragraph, skip it and begin your writing with the second and third paragraph.

TIP 6: Ask the 5 Ws

If you're stuck about how to develop your topic, imagine you're a reporter or a detective, and ask the 5 Ws: *who, what, where, when, why*.

TIP 7: How to Write an Interesting Introduction

- Ask a question, whether or not you answer it right away.
- Use a quotation, which needn't be from a famous person; it might come from someone you've interviewed for the essay.
- Include a startling or shocking fact that will grab your reader's attention.
- Include a dramatic description of a situation or event related to your topic.
- Start out with an exclamation: "Wow! Who knew the problem was this great?" This isn't a question that calls for an answer; it's simply a dramatic device that can often be used effectively. This is called a hypothetical question.

TIP 8: Know the Sentence Structure Rules

- Simple sentences don't have to be short, but they must contain only one independent clause.
- In compound sentences, the two (or more) independent clauses must be related in thought. Do not mix apples and oranges.
- In complex sentences, the dependent clause clarifies the relationship between ideas. Often these dependent clauses start with words like *because, when, who,* or *while.*

TIP 9: Know How to Avoid Common Sentence Structure Errors

- Check every sentence you write for complete thoughts, and for the appropriate subject/verb pairs.
- Read each sentence aloud to see if your voice drops naturally at the end of the sentence. If it doesn't, you've probably written a fragment.
- Slow down. Rushing to get your work finished is a common trap that often produces fragments and/or run-ons.

TIP 10: Avoid Sentence Fragments

- Fragments are allowed only when they are used sparingly for dramatic effect, or to emphasize a point.
- You'll be on safer ground if you obey the rules and avoid using fragments altogether.

TIP 11: Comma Splices Are Common Killers of Good Writing

When in doubt about a comma, leave it out. You have a better chance of conveying meaning without a comma than you do with sticking one in arbitrarily and thereby splicing (or splitting) the sentence unnecessarily.

TIP 12: Use Punctuation Marks Correctly

- Commas and periods always go inside closing quotation marks.
- Question marks go inside or outside quotation marks, depending on your meaning.
- If you are writing dialogue, start a new paragraph for each new speaker.

TIP 13: Avoid the Ellipsis

- Write what you mean; do not depend on the ellipsis to suggest something that you might have written but didn't.
- The only time you should use the ellipsis is to indicate that you have deleted part of a direct quotation.

TIP 14: Avoid the Five Most Common Writing Errors

1. Comma splices are misplaced commas; learning to avoid them and/or correct them is the single most significant improvement you can make in your writing.
2. In every sentence you write, the noun and the verb must agree in number.
3. Verb endings are tricky; they must be checked and used correctly.
4. Pronouns must agree in number, in person, and in function with their antecedent.
5. Misspelling commonly confused words is a common error that can easily be avoided. Rely on a dictionary, not a spell-checker, to check confusing words.

TIP 15: Organize Carefully

Your primary organizational goal is to make it easy for your reader to follow along with you. You must take the reader step by step along the path of your argument.

TIP 16: Your Paragraphs Are Your Building Blocks

- Check and double-check every paragraph of your essay to make sure that each paragraph either supports or expands on your thesis statement.
- Create meaningful transitions between paragraphs; avoid clichéd connecting phrases such as *on the other hand*, *in conclusion*, and *in summary*.

TIP 17: Vary Your Paragraph Length

- A series of very short paragraphs will feel choppy or disconnected, and may be a symptom of a thesis that is not well developed.
- Extremely long paragraphs are difficult to read through—they seem to take the reader's breath away.
- Used carefully, one-sentence paragraphs can make a dramatic impact, but be careful not to overdo this strategy.

TIP 18: Avoid These Bad Writing Habits

- wordiness
- repetitiveness
- clichés and slang
- using a thesaurus to find impressive words
- rushing to finish and therefore making grammatical errors

TIP 19: Adopt the Six Characteristics of Good Writing

1. well-developed ideas and content
2. good organization
3. consistent and appropriate tone and voice
4. powerful and engaging word choice
5. variety in sentence structure
6. correct grammar, spelling, and punctuation

TIP 20: How to Avoid Writer's Block

- Try freewriting or creating a cluster diagram, a mind map, or a rough outline.
- Interview someone connected to your topic.
- Go back and reread the assignment carefully; you may be missing a big clue.
- Give it a rest, overnight if possible, and then come back to your work with fresh eyes the next day.

PRACTICE 1: REVIEWING THE FINAL REVIEW

Reading lists is difficult; everyone tends to skim. For this exercise, go back and reread slowly and carefully the list of tips in this lesson. Highlight in yellow or circle in red the tips that reminded you of problems you have had in your writing.

Once you have created a list of personal problem areas, go back to the table of contents at the beginning of the book and look for the lessons that address your problems. Review those lessons.

Once you've done this review, you're ready to go on to Lesson 30, which provides advice and tips on how to publish your writing.

SECTION 8

publishing your writing

AS A YOUNG writer, you've probably never thought of publishing your writing. Doesn't publishing seem like something only adult, professional writers do? Well, think again.

Actually, every e-mail you write is published—on the Internet. Different forms of published works appear in many places—newspapers, magazines, songs, school bulletin boards, and, of course, books. This final lesson of the book provides you with ideas about where you might find a public place for your writings. Who wouldn't like to see his or her name in print as the author of a well-written essay, poem, or story? Good luck with your writing, and with your publishing, in the future.

seeing your work out in the world

*You must keep sending work out; you must never let
a manuscript do nothing but eat its head off in a drawer.
You send that work out again and again, while you're
working on another one. If you have talent, you will receive
some measure of success—but only if you persist.*

ISAAC ASIMOV (1920–1992)
AMERICAN NOVELIST AND ESSAYIST

Have you ever thought of publishing your writing? Perhaps not, but this lesson
encourages you to reconsider. It's fun to see your name in print, and your teachers and parents will be so proud!

THE ADVICE THAT Isaac Asimov offers here to writers seeking to publish their
work may not seem advice you want to take at this point in your writing life,
but in fact it is excellent advice, even for a writer with modest ambitions. Asimov, who is most famous as a science fiction novelist, published more than 500
books. While you may not have dreams of building a writing career as extensive as Asimov's, publishing your work, right now, is a very real possibility, and
one that you should seriously consider.

For most of Asimov's writing life, publishing meant having his writings
appear printed on paper—in newspapers, magazines, and books. And of course
we usually think of published works as those appearing on paper. However, the

actual definition of *to publish* provides a much wider meaning of the term. Take a look at the dictionary definition:

1. to make information available and distribute it to the public
2. to send forth, as a book, newspaper, musical piece, or other printed work, either for sale or for general distribution; to print, and issue from the press

Publishing, then, is the sending forth of ideas. And that's something you do practically every day of your life. Think about your own use of text messaging, e-mail, and blogs. Every time you use one of those media, you are in fact publishing your ideas, often in very informal ways of course. The ready availability of various electronic media, most notably the Internet, has created amazing new opportunities for writers (and artists) seeking to make their ideas available to others.

HAVE YOU EVER THOUGHT OF PUBLISHING YOUR WRITING?

The answer is probably *No, never!* (Showing your essays to your parents doesn't exactly count as publishing.) Like you, most students think of writing as something they do only for class assignments. Do you think this way? Do you consider that once your essay is written and graded by the teacher, its life is over? Well, think again. You might want to take a bit of Isaac Asimov's advice and try to get something you've written published. Here are some publication ideas to consider.

Local Print Media

1. Submit your best essay (or write a new one) to your school newspaper or to your local community newspaper.
2. Contribute a short story, essay, or poem to a school magazine or to your school's website. If there isn't already a school magazine of student writing, maybe you should start one.
3. Establish a bulletin board in your school hallway where you and other students can post samples of your work.

National Print Media

There are numerous magazines that publish kids' writings; some even sponsor contests with cash prizes. All have websites where you can find the details about how to submit your work. Here's a sampling of some of the best of these print magazines.

1. *Stone Soup* is a magazine made up entirely of the creative work of kids. Young people ages 8 to 13 contribute stories, poems, book reviews, and artwork. www.stonesoup.com

2. *Bookworm*, a magazine by and for kids, was started in 2004 by 11-year-old Sophie McKibben, who wanted to give kids a place to have their writing and art published and shared. http://bookworm-mag.com

3. *Cricket* offers readers cartoons, crossword puzzles, crafts, and recipes created by professional writers. In addition, the magazine runs contests for kids' stories, poetry, art, and photography. www.cricketmag.com/home.asp

4. *New Moon* is a bimonthly magazine created by girls 8 to 12. The magazine, which is free of advertising, is committed to showing girls how to grow into proud, independent women. www.newmoon magazine.org

5. *The Claremont Review*, subtitled *The International Magazine for Young Writers*, is a Canadian magazine that sponsors monthly trivia contests and annual poetry and short story contests for kids. Contest winners have their works published in book form. www.the claremontreview.ca

Online Media

The Internet offers innumerable opportunities for publishing your own work. Here are some great places to start.

1. *KidPub* announces itself as the world's largest online collection of stories written by kids for kids. As members of the site's Authors Club ($12.95 a year), kids are allowed to post new stories, add to a Never-Ending Story, and leave comments for other authors. www.kidpub.com

2. At *Kids.com* you can enter the Write a Story contest immediately. You write your story right there online, and you and other kids vote on the week's submissions. www.kidscom.com/create/write/write.html

3. *Kids Are Authors* is an annual competition open to grades K through 8. Under the guidance of a project coordinator, kids work

in teams of three or more students to write and illustrate their own book. www.scholastic.com/bookfairs/contest/kaa_about.asp

4. At *Merlyn's Pen*, you can submit your writing and actually track your submission as it moves from the e-mail inbox to an editor's desk. Contests include cash prizes and publication on the website. The site publishes fiction, essays, and poems by teens. www .merlynspen.com

5. *The Write Source*, a division of a textbook publisher, accepts submissions of your writing projects (paragraphs, essays, reports, research papers, book reviews, essay-test answers, and other types of nonfiction writing) for possible use in their textbooks. If your work is accepted, you'll receive a $50 savings bond and—if it is published in a handbook or sourcebook—five copies of the book in which your work appears. (Just think, your work could appear in a book just like the one you are reading right now.) www.the writesource.com/publish.htm

Student Writing Contests

1. The National Council of Teachers of English is an organization committed to helping students as well as teachers. Go to their website to find out if your state teachers' association sponsors a contest for student writers. www.ncte.org/about/awards/student/ publish/108196.htm

2. A Utah company called Creative Communication sponsors writing contests for students across the United States and Canada. Multiple contests for different age groups award savings bonds and cash prizes to the winners. www.poeticpower.com

ARE YOU INSPIRED?

Most likely, publishing your writing is a completely new idea for you, but maybe a real possibility now that you've read this list. Remember Isaac Asimov's advice: Keep submitting your work, don't take *no* for an answer—and sooner or later, you too will be a published author. Good luck!

P O S T T E S T

ONCE YOU HAVE completed all the lessons in the book, take this 30-question posttest. This test covers all the material covered in the lessons, and is similar to the pretest, except that the questions are different.

   This test provides you with the opportunity to measure how your writing has improved; your score should be higher on this test. After completing the test and evaluating your score, you may want to go back and review lessons that cover topics with which you had trouble.

   The test should take about 30 minutes to complete. The answer key that follows the test provides the lesson number in which each question's topic is discussed.

POSTTEST

1. Unless otherwise instructed, you should address your writing to whom?
   a. your peer group
   b. the teacher
   c. a general reader
   d. someone like yourself

2. Which of these is the accurate definition of an essay's voice?
   a. the speakers who are quoted in the essay
   b. the expert opinion quoted in the essay
   c. the dialogue used to create atmosphere in the essay
   d. the author's writing style used in the essay

3. Brainstorming is an effective prewriting technique to use in which circumstances?
   a. when you know precisely what you want to write about
   b. when you are given a general, open-ended assignment
   c. when you have only a short amount of time in which to write
   d. when you are planning a particularly long essay

4. Freewriting is a technique best used in which circumstances?
   a. when you are experiencing writer's block
   b. when the assigned topic is open-ended
   c. when you are writing an in-class essay
   d. when you are writing a personal narrative essay

5. Which of these strategies is likely to be most useful in determining an essay's conclusion?
   a. freewriting
   b. brainstorming
   c. outlining
   d. concept mapping

6. An essay's thesis statement usually appears where?
   a. in the first or second paragraph
   b. in the first paragraph always
   c. in each supporting paragraph
   d. in the conclusion

7. What are the 5 W questions used frequently by journalists and other writers?
   a. *who, what, where, when, why*
   b. *who, which, where, when, why*
   c. *which, why, where, whatever, whose*
   d. *who, which, whose, when, why*

8. A useful essay template to use in multiple circumstances is which of these?
   a. the three-paragraph essay
   b. the five-paragraph essay
   c. the comparison-contrast essay
   d. the narrative or personal essay

9. The body paragraphs in an essay perform which function(s)?
   a. offer counterarguments to your thesis
   b. offer supporting evidence for your thesis
   c. offer both **a** and **b**
   d. offer your conclusions

10. A topic sentence should appear where?
   a. in the concluding paragraph
   b. in every paragraph
   c. in the first paragraph
   d. in both **a** and **c**

11. Which of these is a strong organizational strategy for a persuasive essay?
   a. cause and effect
   b. order of importance (least to most)
   c. order of importance (most to least)
   d. compare and contrast

12. Which feature is a good addition to an essay's conclusions?
   a. an appeal to the reader's emotions
   b. an expansion of the thesis statement
   c. both **a** and **b**
   d. an additional related idea

13. When you are writing an in-class essay, most of your time should be spent
    a. drafting.
    b. proofreading.
    c. editing.
    d. outlining.

14. The outlining process should occur
    a. after brainstorming.
    b. before drafting.
    c. before establishing your thesis.
    d. all of the above

15. Which is the most reliable way to proofread your essay?
    a. Have a smart friend read it.
    b. Have a parent read it.
    c. Use your computer's spell-checker.
    d. Read it aloud very slowly.

16. What is the main problem with the following sentence?
        After putting off her homework for the entire weekend Sally decided
        on Sunday night to get down to work and write fast.
    a. It is not properly punctuated.
    b. It is ungrammatical.
    c. It is wordy.
    d. It is a run-on sentence.

17. What is the main problem with the following sentence?
        The sixth-grade boys organized there club into two opposing
        groups; each group chose a mascot.
    a. It is not properly punctuated.
    b. It is wordy.
    c. It contains a pronoun error.
    d. It is a run-on sentence.

18. What is the main problem with the following sentence?

> Learning to write is difficult especially when you approach the idea of writing with preconceived notions about what is fun and what is not so much fun and then you let those ideas influence you.

   a. It contains verb errors.

   b. It is a run-on sentence.

   c. It is wordy.

   d. It contains spelling errors.

19. Which of the following organizational strategies would work best for an essay on how to fix a flat tire on a bicycle?

   a. chronological

   b. persuasive

   c. compare-contrast

   d. problem/solution

20. Which of the following is the strongest thesis statement for a persuasive essay?

   a. Skateboarding is challenging and difficult.

   b. Skateboarding is the most popular sport among my friends.

   c. Skateboarding is a growing trend.

   d. Skateboarding should be outlawed in our town.

21. Which of the following is the weakest thesis statement for a persuasive essay?

   a. Skateboarding is challenging and difficult.

   b. Skateboarding is the most popular sport among my friends.

   c. Skateboarding is a growing trend.

   d. Skateboarding should be outlawed in our town.

22. Which of the following sentences has the most effective word choice?

   a. Skateboarding is challenging and difficult.

   b. Skateboarding is terrifying but fun.

   c. Skateboarding is an extremely popular sport.

   d. Skateboarding is not for sissies.

3. The first part of your planning time should be
   a. brainstorming.
   b. outlining.
   c. analyzing the prompt.
   d. freewriting.

24. Identify the error in the following sentence.
      Harry and Sally have met before when they went to a different
      school.
   a. spelling error
   b. verb error
   c. pronoun error
   d. none of the above

25. Identify the error in the following sentence.
      Either baseball or basketball are the most popular sport with most
      kids.
   a. spelling error
   b. noun error
   c. verb error
   d. none of the above

26. Identify the error in the following sentence.
      Each girl had their tap shoes stuffed in their backpack.
   a. spelling error
   b. verb error
   c. pronoun error
   d. none of the above

27. Identify the error in the following sentence.
      When we were in first grade, we will learn that the planets revolved
      around the sun.
   a. spelling error
   b. verb error
   c. pronoun error
   d. none of the above

28. Identify the error in the following sentence.

> The computer was universally adopted, typewriters became antiques, that nobody wanted.

a. spelling error

b. verb error

c. noun error

d. comma splice

29. Identify the error in the following sentence.

> You feel its time for a break when the test gets to it's end.

a. verb error

b. noun error

c. pronoun error

d. comma splice

30. Identify the error in the following sentence.

> Half the questions was easy, but the other half was really difficult.

a. noun error

b. verb error

c. comma splice

d. none of the above

ANSWERS

1. **c** (Lesson 7)
2. **d** (Lesson 7)
3. **b** (Lesson 8)
4. **a** (Lesson 10)
5. **c** (Lesson 14)
6. **a** (Lesson 12)
7. **a** (Lesson 11)
8. **b** (Lesson 21)
9. **c** (Lesson 21)
10. **b** (Lesson 11)
11. **b** (Lesson 15)
12. **c** (Lesson 23)
13. **a** (Lesson 19)
14. **d** (Lesson 14)
15. **d** (Lesson 28)
16. **a** (Lesson 4)
17. **c** (Lesson 3)
18. **b** (Lessons 2, 6)
19. **d** (Lesson 15)
20. **d** (Lesson 12)
21. **b** (Lesson 12)
22. **b** (Lesson 10)
23. **c** (Lesson 17)
24. **b** (Lesson 6)
25. **c** (Lesson 6)
26. **c** (Lesson 3)
27. **b** (Lesson 6)
28. **d** (Lesson 6)
29. **c** (Lesson 3)
30. **b** (Lesson 6)

action verb   a verb that expresses thought or activity

adjective   a word that modifies a noun or a pronoun; adjectives answer *what kind? which one? how much? how many?* about a noun

adverb   a word that modifies a verb, an adjective, or another adverb; adverbs answer *where? when? how much? how many?* about the verb, adjective, or other adverb

chronological order   an organizational structure that presents events in sequence, or in the time order in which they happened

colon (:)   the punctuation mark that comes before a series, a lengthy quotation, or an example, or after the salutation in a business letter

comma (,)   the punctuation mark that separates words, phrases, and items in a series; commas are also used in compound and complex sentences to separate clauses

compare   to look for ways in which things are alike

complex sentence a sentence that is made up of an independent clause and a dependent (subordinate) clause

compound-complex sentence a sentence that is made up of more than one independent clause and at least one dependent clause

compound sentence a sentence that contains at least two independent clauses with no dependent clauses

compound subject two or more nouns that share the same verb in a sentence

compound word two or more separate words put together to create a new word; compound words may be joined, separate, or hyphenated (see also *portmanteau word*)

conclusion the final paragraph (or paragraphs) in an essay, which restates the main idea, summarizes the main points, and closes, sometimes with a call to action or an appeal to the reader's emotions

conjunction a word or phrase (*and, or, but*) that connects words or groups of words

contrast to show how things or ideas are different

dangling modifier a word or phrase that is meant to modify a specific part of the sentence, but has been misplaced, often resulting in confusion

demonstrative pronoun a word (such as *this, that, these,* and *those*) used to replace a noun in a sentence

dependent clause a group of words that cannot stand alone as a complete thought; also known as a *subordinate clause*

direct object the noun or pronoun that receives the action of the verb

direct quotation a person's exact spoken or written words, which must be enclosed in quotation marks (see also *indirect quotation*)

effect what happens as a result of something else

emoticon the typed representation of a facial expression; often used in e-mails

emotional appeal an argument that appeals to the reader's emotions

exclamation point (!) the punctuation mark that indicates strong emotion

first person writing in which the author (or a narrator in a short story) speaks in his or her own voice

freewriting the practice of writing continuously without correcting spelling, grammar, or sentence structure to facilitate finding a topic or increase fluency; also called *prewriting*

future tense   a verb tense that indicates that something has not yet happened, but will

hyphen (-)   the punctuation mark that joins or separates numbers, letters, or syllables

indefinite pronoun   a word such as *no one, anyone, anybody,* or *somebody* that refers to a nonspecific noun

independent clause   a group of words that contains a subject and a predicate (verb) and can stand by itself as a sentence

indirect quotation   what someone said, retold in your own words

infinitive   a verb written in the form of *to* plus the verb (for example, *to walk*) that acts as a noun, an adjective, or an adverb in a sentence

interrogative pronouns   a pronoun that asks *who, whom, whose,* and so on

introduction   an essay's opening paragraph that hooks the reader and introduces the thesis statement

literature   a form of writing that includes poems, novels, short stories, and plays

main idea   what a selection is mostly about

misplaced modifier   a word or phrase that is placed too far from the noun or verb it is modifying, thus altering or confusing the meaning of the sentence

modifier   a word that describes or clarifies another word (see also *adjective* and *adverb*)

noun   a word that names a person, place, or thing (including ideas and feelings)

object of a preposition   the noun or pronoun that follows a prepositional phrase

order of importance   an organizational strategy that arranges ideas according to how important they are

parentheses [( )]   the punctuation marks that set off information that is not necessarily pertinent to the surrounding sentence or words

participle   a verb form that can be used as an adjective or a noun

past tense   a verb tense that indicates that something has already happened

period (.)   the punctuation mark found at the end of sentences and in abbreviations

personal pronoun   a word such as *I, you, me, he, him, she, her, it, they, them,* and *we* that refer to the speaker, the person, or the thing being spoken about

phrase   a group of words that does not have a subject and verb; phrases can act like various parts of speech (a noun, a verb, an adjective, an adverb, or a preposition)

point of view   the first-person, second-person, or third-person perspective from which something is written, or the opinion or position on a topic from which an author writes

portmanteau word   a new word formed by combining two words (for example, *blog* is formed from *web* and *log*)

predicate   the action that the subject performs in a sentence; a verb

present tense   a verb tense that indicates action happening in the present or an action that happens constantly

prewriting   the practice of writing continuously without correcting spelling, grammar, or sentence structure to facilitate finding a topic or increase fluency; also called *freewriting*

pronoun   a part of speech that takes the place of a noun in a sentence

proper noun   a specific noun that is capitalized

punctuation   a set of grammatical symbols used in written language to indicate the ends of clauses or sentences

question mark (?)   the punctuation mark that appears at the end of an interrogatory sentence (a question)

quotation marks (" ")   the punctuation marks that indicate the exact words of a speaker being quoted; sometimes quotation marks are used to convey a satiric or ironic intent in the author's words

run-on sentence   a sentence in which two or more complete sentences have been improperly joined together

second person   a point of view in which the reader is referred to as *you*

semicolon (;)   the punctuation mark that joins two independent clauses that share a similar idea and are not already joined by a conjunction

sentence   a group of words that has a subject and a predicate and expresses a complete thought

sentence fragment   an incomplete thought that has been punctuated as a complete sentence

sentence structure   the various kinds of sentences an author uses

simple sentence   an independent clause

subject   topic, or what the text is about; also, the grammatical term for the main noun in a sentence

subject-verb agreement   the rule that the subject and verb of a sentence must agree in number and in person

subordinate clause   a group of words that cannot stand alone as a complete thought; also known as a *dependent clause*

theme   the main message or messages that a piece of literature promotes; a story can have multiple themes

thesis   a statement in an essay that conveys the main idea

third person   a point of view in which the author speaks in an impersonal tone or in which the narrator of a short story is not a character in the story

tone   the writer's style that reveals the attitudes and point of view of the author toward the topic

topic   the subject or main idea of an essay or a paragraph

topic sentence   a sentence that expresses the main idea of a paragraph

verb   a part of speech that expresses action or state of being. The tense of a verb indicates the time in which the verb takes place.